Kris~

All the best to you and your family.

xo

Cathy

We have known Cathy for years and have seen her help many struggling families through their darkest times. Her skill and kindness shine through in this book—she is truly committed to helping families impacted by substance use. If you are a parent or a loved one looking for guidance, this book will offer insight, compassion, and a friend to guide you through this struggle.

–Jeff Foote, PhD, Co-Founder of CMC: Foundation for Change and The Center for Motivation and Change

An informative and personal narrative that shows how evidence-supported practices and caring relationships can open the door for, and support, a loved one's recovery. This is an important resource for families looking to help their loved one, have permission to do so in a way that aligns with their values, and feel supported through the wisdom of Ms. Taughinbaugh's lived experience.

–Ken Carpenter, PhD, CMC: Foundation for Change and The Center for Motivation and Change

Cathy Taughinbaugh's book is an appreciated addition to the limited library of books about CRAFT and other relationship-positive approaches to addiction. Drawing from her experience using CRAFT with families, she provides many helpful case examples and nuggets of wisdom about how the concepts apply in real life.

–Lara Okoloko, MSW, Certified CRAFT Clinician

Within the pages of The Compassion Antidote: A Path to Change for You and Your Child Struggling with Substance Use, Cathy Taughinbaugh shares her wisdom, warmth, help, and hope for parents trying to find their way on one of life's most difficult journeys. As a parent who has walked this walk herself—and as a certified parent coach—Cathy skillfully empowers parents with her straightforward and evidence-based approach to constructive change. This little book is a gem, one that parents will want to keep close at hand....every step of the way.

–Sandy Swenson, parent advocate and author of *The Joey Song: A Mother's Story of Her Son's Addiction*

"If you have a child who struggles with a substance use disorder - whether they be an adolescent or an adult - Cathy Taughinbaugh's latest book, *The Compassion Antidote,* is a must-read. As a mother who has dealt with substance use disorders, Cathy understands where you are at. Searching for answers, she spent years interviewing experts and studying evidence-based research on addiction, what it takes to treat it, and how a parent can best support their child through that journey. To that end, she trained in the CRAFT program and was one of the first CRAFT-trained parent recovery coaches for the Partnership to End Addiction. Filled with the personal experiences, anecdotes, and case studies of the parents she's coached over the past ten years, Cathy offers a myriad of suggestions to help parents help their children *and* themselves."

–Lisa Frederiksen, author of *The 10th Anniversary Edition If You Loved Me, You'd Stop!* and founder of Breaking the Cycles

In "The Compassion Antidote," Cathy braids together the wisdom she gained as a mom practicing CRAFT in her own home and the experiences of other parents who have also used the approach with the expertise of great minds such as Drs Jeff Foote, Carrie Wilson, and Nicole Kosanke of the Center for Motivation and Change; Thich Nat Hanh, Dan Harris, Dr. Gabor Mate, Dr. Kristen Neff, Dr. Russ Harris, and of course, Dr. Meyers and colleagues who developed CRAFT.

Cathy's book is a balance of warmth, compassion, practicality, and simplicity. While reading, I found some sentences that I wish I could have offered to myself years ago in my journey as a mom and other sentences that I want to provide to the families I work with as a CRAFT clinician now.

She gives a name to parents' struggles, lets them know that they are not alone, and that, in a world where confrontation often gets the spotlight....that there is another way. Thank you for sharing your experiences with CRAFT!

–Cordelia Kraus, LPC, CADC 1, Certified CRAFT Clinician

Cathy's user-friendly book gives the reader insights on how to help their teen or young adult using evidence-based practices. The book shares the critical role that family plays in finding solutions when it comes to addiction. *The Compassion Antidote* reminds the reader that they are not alone, offers hope and a way forward.

–Denise Mariano, Director, Family Support and Advocacy, Partnership to End Addiction

The book wonderfully summarized the possibilities and successes of using CRAFT methodologies.

–Ron Grover, parent advocate and blogger at An Addict in Our Son's Bedroom

'Take Heart, Compassion, Changing the Conversation'; as a member of a family with addiction, Ms. Taughinbaugh's chapter titles strike deep into my heart and soul. Her chapter summaries include such nuggets as "One size doesn't fit all when it comes to addiction. Bravo!

–Patrick Doyle LICSW, Family Addiction Coach

Like many families, when addiction entered our home, we were thrust into an unfamiliar and scary world. We were encouraged to detach, but that didn't feel right for us. *The Compassion Antidote* offers parents an approach more aligned with their instincts to support their children through life's challenges instead of letting go. Cathy Taughinbaugh provides a valuable resource to help parents stay connected to their struggling children, bring harmony back to the home, and create the conditions that will nudge their loved ones toward recovery. It is essential reading for parents who need help and hope.

–Rose Barbour, parent of two sons in long-term recovery and an addiction advocate, writer, and blogger.

THE Compassion ANTIDOTE

A Path to Change for You and Your Child Struggling with Substance Use

Catherine Taughinbaugh

The Compassion Antidote

A Path to Change for You and Your Child Struggling with Substance Use

By Catherine Taughinbaugh

Print ISBN: 978-1-66781-076-8

ebook ISBN: 978-1-66781-077-5

Printed in the United States of America.

Editor: Teja Watson

DISCLAIMER

The purpose of this book is to provide general information. Every effort has been made to supply accurate information, citation, and credit sources to the reader. The information provided here represents the author's experiences and reference material and is not intended as medical advice or a substitute for professional advice, treatment, and guidance. You should not use this information to diagnose or treat a health problem or disease without consulting a qualified health care professional or expert. The author and publisher shall have neither liability nor responsibility to any injury, loss, or damage caused or alleged to have been caused directly or indirectly by the information in this book. The stories in this book are composites of actual situations. Any resemblance to specific persons, living or dead, or specific events is entirely coincidental. Much of this book is based on the author's interpretation and experience with the Community Reinforcement and Family Training (CRAFT) approach. No guarantees, explicit or implied, are given that the reader will have an outcome similar to any experiences described in this book.

TABLE OF CONTENTS

To every parent who has been touched
by their child's substance use.
And to my children, who have been
my greatest teachers.

INTRODUCTION

It's never too late to be who you might have been. —*George Eliot*

I have comfort in knowing that someone out there can relate, someone that knows this problem is not just black and white, but most issues are in this huge gray area. —*Cyndi F.*

Our country is currently dealing with the most difficult challenges around drug and alcohol use that it has ever seen. Chances are, you know how it feels to have a son or daughter struggling with substance use.

You may have discovered that your child is smoking pot, taking pills, engaging in underage drinking, or addicted to heroin. Trying to cope with these issues can be the worst thing you've gone through as a parent. It can create fear, frustration, anger, and pain for all involved.

According to the National Association of Treatment Providers, "In 2019, 19.3 million (7.7%) people in the US aged 18 or older had a substance use disorder (SUD)." So if you and your child are experiencing this pain, know that you are not alone! These words from other struggling parents may resonate with you.

"Our youngest is our son, who is twenty-one years old and has been struggling with substance use since he was sixteen. There have been numerous arrests for stealing, juvenile drug court, and adult felony charges currently pending."

"My daughter is twenty-six years old and is addicted to alcohol. She went to a sober living home and drank the second night after having been sober for almost six months."

"My twenty-eight-year-old is once again in jail for marijuana and crystal meth, disorderly conduct, and threatening messages. He has been to so many rehabs I can't keep count. It's hard for me to stop enabling him."

When the substance use started, you may not have had any idea what was going on. Once you became aware of the problem, you probably did the best you could to find answers. If you're like most parents, those answers weren't always easy to come by—but with some effort you can find your way.

Addiction is a complicated problem. One answer does not work for every situation. Your child is an individual, a unique human being who turned to substances because of anxiety, depression, trauma, or other reasons. And while some struggle in silence for many years, it's crucial for you and your child to know that you're not alone.

In this book, I want to share my experiences, the experiences of other parents I've worked with, and information I've learned along the way. *The Compassion Antidote* is about bridging the gap between feeling helpless and healing—having a beacon of light to lead you and your family down the path. It's a practical guide to moving past overwhelming fear, frustration, anger, and pain, from a parents' perspective.

This book is for parents, and I use that term throughout the book. However, the term *parent* is meant to include grandparents, aunts, uncles, other family members and caregivers who are trying to understand the problem and help in any way that they can.

I want this book to be inclusive to all. So, no matter what your background, my hope is that you can find some ideas that make sense for you. We all need to work together to help our kids find their way to a healthy lifestyle.

Many parents and other family members have learned skills to help themselves. There are lots of examples of people throughout the world who have overcome their unique challenges, developed their inner strength, and built a life of meaning and purpose.

Take Heart

If your child is struggling with drugs or alcohol, I've been where you are now. I understand your feelings of despair and worry, the frustration and emotional turmoil you may be feeling.

My hope is that what I've learned in my journey as a parent and as a coach will help you support your child. I've gathered information from addiction professionals, other parents, support groups, and books.

My training in Community Reinforcement and Family Training (CRAFT) has dramatically influenced my work with parents. The idea of having research behind the approach makes so much sense to me. And the idea of approaching addiction as a health issue that is more likely to improve with compassionate care supports families in the best way possible.

You will find here a variety of ideas to help you navigate the choppy waters of your child's drug or alcohol use, and my desire is that the stories and information will inspire you to keep moving forward in a positive direction. As you read, take note of what information you connect with, what feels right for your family, and what is doable for you. Educate yourself, but listen to your heart.

The most important thing you can do is not give up on your child. Everyone has the potential to recover. Your child *can* change and live a better life. May they go forward and join the millions in recovery!

Catherine Taughinbaugh

Certified Parent Coach

CathyTaughinbaugh.com

PART 1:
TAKE HEART

CHAPTER 1

The Beginning

I can't change anyone's behavior, but I can influence that behavior by my actions. —Robert J. Meyers

I'm on the same journey as the rest of you. Ups and downs. Hopes and fears. —Kathy W.

Growing up with my parents and my three older brothers, I don't remember experiencing my family members having an issue with alcohol. My parents seemed very conscious of not drinking too much.

My dad had been married once before he married my mom. His first wife, Judy, struggled with alcohol—so my two older brothers from my dad's first marriage had a very different experience. One of my brothers, who wrote a book for his family, said:

"My memories of those days are of survival in the midst of chaos. We were on our own and we made the best of it. There were drunken parties, fights, broken heads, and the frequent visits by the police. Mother was happy and carefree until she got drunk, and then she would be a mean drunk. We tried our best to stay out of harm's way. There was an outside door to our bedroom, which was sometimes used as an entrance by strangers and as an escape hatch for us. We were often scared at night and would hide in the closet, fall asleep, and not wake up until the next morning. We were at times alone in the house for days."

I have to give my dad credit for intervening. He was transferred to Indiana from California in 1949 soon after he married my mom and he insisted on taking his two sons, who were ten and twelve at the time, with him. Judy had legal custody, so this was technically kidnapping, yet he was willing to take that chance because he believed his sons would be safer with him. They lived with us in Indiana, and later after our move back to California, until they went to college. While I'm sure it was traumatic for them to leave their mother, whom they didn't see for four years, they were both successful in life and neither has had any issues with alcohol. This was during a time when there was very little help or resources for alcohol dependence.

I tried drinking several times in high school. A group of us went on a YMCA trip to Lake Havasu my senior year. Someone had snuck some beer along, and of course I had to give it a try. I enjoyed the risk taking. I didn't love the taste, however, so it wasn't something I turned to as a habit. From that first experience of drinking alcohol with friends, I thought of it as something fun to do on the weekends. Most of my friends and I drank in college when we were ready to kick back.

It was the 1970s, and marijuana and harder drugs were prevalent. Yet I knew of no one taking pills, heroin, meth, or any of the other riskier drugs. Many of us experimented with alcohol or marijuana at parties, but it was minimal. We had fun and sometimes pushed the limits, but thankfully didn't do anything to ruin our lives. Things seemed less complicated back then.

I was lucky that my alcohol and drug use didn't open a Pandora's box. I had fun, but my life never revolved around getting my next drink or my next high. Like most people, as an adult, I've had my ups and downs, but I have never felt that I needed substances to get through my day.

When I became a mother, I expected that my kids would follow a similar path, even though drug and alcohol use was more common when my kids were teenagers. I knew the teen years might be challenging, but I figured they were a phase that would pass. My children would muddle through, shake off their teenage angst as I did, and find their place in the world. They would grow into healthy adults and find meaningful work, good friends, and love. I never dreamed that their lives would be shackled with the burden of drug use, which would evolve into dependence and addiction.

Instead, I've had to live through the despair and helplessness that come with watching your child make devastating choices, from excessive marijuana use to crystal meth use. For many years, I believed that I was responsible for their substance use. It was my job, yet I wasn't able to guide my kids in a better direction. Addiction had touched our family because, as a parent, I had done something wrong.

Like other parents, I felt the stigma and judgment around drug use and was hesitant to speak up. I feared friends and neighbors discovering our shameful secrets. I experienced the pain of divorce, which affected me and my children. While their early years were positive in many ways, having their family uprooted by divorce most likely played a role in their later substance use. While it was hard, I am grateful we were able to agree on custody. My kids' dad and I were both involved in their lives and they spent a good deal of time with both of us throughout their childhood, which was a good thing. Like many families, we have some addiction genetics in our family background. But they each had their own reasons for turning to drugs to numb the pain of their feelings.

The most frightening part is that there is no instruction manual on dealing with this. Information can be conflicting and confusing. It isn't easy to know where to turn and what information to trust. While we may want to believe that a crisis can bring families together, the longer addiction goes on, the easier it is for families to fall apart.

Reaching Out

As time went on, I attended several 12-step support groups to get help. As I met more parents with struggling children through these groups, I was touched by what their families were going through.

I had been an educator in an elementary school for fifteen years and had recently retired from teaching. Now was the perfect time for me to take on another project. I knew how confused I had been when I first learned my kids had drug problems. Sharing ideas with other parents seemed like the right thing to do.

We were eventually able to enlist the help of two treatment centers (one sober living facility, one interventionist) and therapy for my kids. I worked hard to let go of blaming myself for things that weren't perfect. After my daughter and son had been doing well for a few years, I decided to create a website. I've always loved technology, so creating a website and connecting online intrigued me.

I have always loved psychology, too. I became fascinated by trying to understand what makes a person turn to substances and then not be able to stop. It seemed wrong that so many young people were losing their dreams for their future, or even their lives. I became passionate about the topic, and my work became therapy for me. I wanted it to be a beacon of hope for other parents who were as confused and frustrated as I had been.

I started reading other parent blogs on the same topic. One I found early on was Ron Grover's "An Addict in Our Son's Bedroom." Someone from the Partnership to End Addiction read a comment I had left on Ron's blog, and I was asked to become a parent volunteer for the Partnership's parent network.

In 2013, the Partnership offered its first training for volunteer parent coaches. Psychologists would teach this training from the Center for Motivation and Change in New York City in August. I was interested in participating; I had already decided that I wanted to work with other parents, so this seemed like a perfect fit. So I was off to New York as part of the charter group of eleven parent partners to be trained by Jeff Foote and his team. What wisdom and foresight these two organizations had! Their efforts have helped parents find their way and saved countless lives.

Community Reinforcement and Family Training (CRAFT) was developed by Robert J. Meyers, PhD, who is the director of Robert J. Meyers, PhD and Associates and a research associate professor emeritus in Psychology at the University of New Mexico's Center on Alcoholism, Substance Abuse, and Addictions. While CRAFT was designed for anyone who has a misuser resistant to treatment, the pilot program in New York was focused on training parents on the research-based tools and strategies that they could use at home to help their struggling teen or young adult. As parents, we learned so much from the training, which none of us had ever heard about before.

It was great to meet Ron Grover and the other parent participants. Ron explains his thoughts on the training this way: "I learned so much about helping other parents living the life I lived for so long. What was amazing was exactly how much sense everything made in Jeff's presentation and how well it worked. Those days, all eleven of us learned so much from Jeff and his team but we also learned so much from each other. To say those days were life-changing would be an understatement. So much credit goes to Tom Hendrick and the Partnership. They were the ones with the foresight to bring all this to fruition for so many."

My entire outlook on how a parent could help their child through addiction and recovery changed. Like many parents, I had been told there was nothing I could do to help, and I needed to let go. From this training, I learned that parents *could* use strategies that would help motivate their children to change. A door to a new way of thinking opened.

I've learned from the work of other experts too, especially those providing evidence-based, compassionate approaches. I've learned to pick and choose what would work for our family and help parents find what will work for their situation. The underlying mindset of all of them is that substance use is a problem that needs a well-researched approach, coupled with compassion and kindness.

A New Paradigm

Too many parents hear that there is only one solution to their child's addiction: to step away. They are told that if they want to help their kids, they are enablers or they are codependent. But the truth is, you *can* help your children in a healthy way.

Through the years, countless parents have told me that they were not comfortable with letting go of their child. They didn't want to sit on the sidelines and wait for their child to hit rock bottom. I couldn't imagine turning my back on my children either. The stress alone, of not knowing where they were or how they were doing, would be too much. It made so much more sense to me to come at the problem in a more positive way. I wanted to have things I *could* do. I discovered that parents don't have to turn their backs on their kids; we can help them help themselves. This has been a relief to me and other parents I've talked to and worked with.

With CRAFT and through my experience, I've come to realize that one size doesn't fit all. My children felt the need to use substances for different reasons, and they've changed their lives at their own pace, in their own way. While there are similarities, each situation, individual, and family is different.

The tide is changing. As new research comes to the forefront, more options are available. Yet many are still struggling. Addiction is still rearing its ugly head throughout our country. There is much work to be done.

Our children need to be motivated by something in order to want to change their life. The magic sauce of CRAFT is that by changing how you approach your child and the words you use, and by topping your approach with kindness and compassion, you can create the foundation that motivates your child to want to change. Parents can guide their adult children or teens to see the value of getting help and living a healthier life. You can show them the way.

We can be a positive force through the way we talk, react, and approach the problem. Parents have more influence than most people realize. Yelling and being confrontational—or detaching and letting go—prove not to be so helpful.

I've experienced the world of substance use for more than fifteen years. As I've worked with parents as they try to better cope with the heartache of watching their children become dependent on drugs or alcohol, what became clear was their relief that there are options. They didn't have to let go of their children. With knowledge and understanding, we can find our way towards a more compassionate approach. I've watched parents evolve and change, which then filtered down to their children. And that is why I wanted to share these ideas and write this book.

Real change comes from showing our children how much we love them, seeing them for who they are, and understanding why they turned to drugs in the first place. We can be more self-aware, and change ourselves first, which will in turn help our children. When we stay with our children through the despair, fear and frustration, we help them see how strong they are.

Chapter Summary

- Times are different now for our kids than when we were growing up.
- Parents can be caught off guard when they don't have an issue with alcohol or drugs and they discover their children do.
- CRAFT introduces a compassionate, kind way to help your child change.
- One size doesn't fit all when it comes to addiction.
- Helping your child starts with understanding the root of the problem.

CHAPTER 2

The Problem

There's no hole too deep for a person to dig themselves out of with the right support, with the right help, with the right tools and with the right self-belief. —Dr. Adi Jaffe

In my work as a court reporter, I see the impact drugs have on families, children, and communities. It is devastating, and it is certainly an epidemic. —Brenda L.

Today, families of all sorts and sizes have experienced substance use with their kids—there is no discrimination. Intact and divorced, affluent and poor, inner-city and suburban—too many families are experiencing the devastation of watching their children travel down this dark road.

Addiction affects every facet of family life, with parents bearing the brunt of the toll. They worry the most, sleep the least, and feel the most shame and anxiety. And then there's the sad truth that, while many people do eventually recover from their drug or alcohol dependence, there are too many online memorials of young people who have lost their lives to an overdose. Parents bear that heavy burden as well.

It's a sad fact that my article "When Addiction Wins" is one of the most read and commented on articles on my blog. The drug problem in the United States is not new; however, its rise in the rankings as a cause of death is alarming.

This means that what had been a personal problem for some is now a significant issue for diverse communities worldwide. We need answers. Substance use is stealing the dreams and—too often—the lives of our children.

Where It Often Begins: Teen Substance Use

Children are using drugs at earlier and earlier ages. They take their first drink or their first drug to see how it makes them feel, or because of peer pressure. They assume that they can control how much they use. They never dream that it will prevent them from living their life. But drugs and alcohol can take away a person's ability to choose, because they change the brain.

Over time, continued use of drugs or alcohol changes your brain—in dramatic and dangerous or even subtle ways, but nearly always in ways that encourage compulsive and often uncontrollable use, despite the many adverse effects. Drug addiction compels a person to become obsessed with obtaining and using substances. As time passes and your child continues to use, their habit goes from being voluntary to compulsive. It can affect their brain development and the trajectory of their life if they become dependent.

But there is much more going on. Drug or alcohol use is an expression of a deeper problem.

According to the Partnership to End Addiction, "Ninety percent of people with addictions started using substances in their teen years. Beginning at age 10 through the mid-to-late-20s, massive changes are underway in the brain. This includes the development of capabilities related to impulse control, managing emotions, problem-solving and anticipating consequences. Substance use during this time period can prime the brain to be more susceptible to addiction and other mental health disorders, especially for kids who are vulnerable."

Understanding and Compassion Helps Begin the Healing Process

If you suspect your child is experimenting with drugs, one of the first steps is to take a deeper look at what is going on. Why is he or she turning to drugs? Your child may be curious about what drug or alcohol use is all about or feel the peer pressure to give it a try. For others, substance use is an escape or a way to solve a problem.

Whatever their reason, ask yourself: What is working in my communication with my child, and what is not? You can help by listening to what your son or daughter is going through without judging them. Try to get a clear understanding of what is enticing them to want to use drugs or alcohol. When you understand the motivation, you can get to the root of the problem.

The Day Begins and Ends with Worry

Parents are affected when a child is engaging in drug or alcohol misuse. But it is hard for some—if not all—parents to accept the unbearable truth that their child is using substances.

While I had hoped things were going well with my kids, by the end of high school, I noticed that my daughter was not herself. My son, too, experimented a few years earlier, during his teen years. They did an excellent job of covering it up. Their experimentation would lead to crystal meth and daily dependence on marijuana.

It's easy at first to refuse to believe that your child is experimenting or even has become dependent on substances. Denial is a mental defense mechanism, to help us cope with knowledge we are not ready to accept. Once a parent is prepared to deal with the problem, finding answers becomes their sole aim.

It is genuinely torturous going through addiction with your child. You may feel hopeless as you watch your son or daughter continue to use substances and not be able to stop, no matter how hard they try.

Yet it is equally challenging to do what so many recommend: cut them out of your life. *Cut my kid out of my life?!?* It's unnatural for a parent to turn their back on a child, whether they're fifteen or thirty. And yet that is the advice parents are so often given, which only creates more stress.

As time drags on without resolution, parents often second-guess themselves. Three moms expressed it in these ways:

"It feels like our family is 'broken.' There are so many feelings that I don't know how to deal with: fear, anger, worry, frustration, and sadness toward my son's drinking behaviors that could negatively impact just about every aspect of his life."

"I feel like a failure. I worry and obsess about my daughter's health, safety, and happiness all the time. I feel ashamed of the pain that this has caused our family. It's hard to watch the self-destruction. I do not sleep well when I am worrying."

"I struggle most with wondering how I could have missed the fact that my son was using drugs. I thought that because we have such a close relationship, I would have realized it sooner."

When you add in regret, this can become a truly toxic stew. One regret I have is not sending my kids to counseling soon after our divorce. I don't know if that would have made a difference, but it would have at least given them a safe place to share their feelings about what was going on in our family. I feel I missed the boat on that one. They seemed to be doing well, or so I told myself.

Another mom I worked with regretted that her son had started using drugs when his dad died. He wasn't able to cope well. She wished she had been more aware of his grief and in tune with his loss. Some parents feel they did all the right things, and their child still went down that dark road.

As the worry, work, and expenses mount, parents can feel mentally, physically, psychologically, and emotionally exhausted. I can hear it in their voices and feel it in the tone they use. They are scared, frustrated, and angry and want answers. Their day begins and ends with worry.

Strain, Stress, and Grief

Parents can spend years of ups and downs, trying to find a way to cope. They may struggle to feel productive in their work or relationships. It is easy to lose your joy for life when you are constantly worrying about your child. Many become obsessed with wanting to fix their son or daughter. It can become a long journey for all involved.

One mom wrote me, asking for help. "It consumed me for two long years to the point where I couldn't function. How do I know what to do and not to do when it comes to my son's drug use? I'm doing a little better now because I have done a lot of research, but I still have days where it floors me."

Another wrote, "My daughter's use has left me feeling unsure. I am at a loss, and my nerves are frayed. I feel worried and anxious. I want to see my daughter back on track." Parents feel helpless as they watch their children wander further down the path of drug use. As one mom put it, "It's sucking the life out of me."

For some, the overwhelming feeling is sadness. One woman's son had done well academically in the past but had since lost his bright future. The loss of their child's potential and their dream for their child fills parents with grief.

The Myth of Enabling

Parents find themselves under tremendous stress when trying to cope with their child's substance use. Many are concerned about knowing when they've overstepped boundaries, helped too much, or unintentionally supported their child's continued use.

But most aren't aware that their actions sometimes enable the child to continue their drug use. They don't want to enable their child, but saying no is challenging. And spouses or partners can become frustrated with each other. One parent can instill firm boundaries, while the other parent has a hard time doing so. One dad asked, "How can I get my wife to stop enabling our son?" And plenty of moms are frustrated because their husbands or partners step in with money or other things that kick the can down the road and prolong the struggle.

However, the term "enabler" has negative connotations. Parents in this situation don't need another reason to feel bad about themselves. So please refrain from labeling yourself or someone else as an enabler. Most parents are doing the best they can in a difficult situation.

We blame ourselves for being too strict, too lenient, too passive, too busy, too emotional. There is no such thing as perfect parenting, and being an imperfect parent doesn't necessarily create a child with substance use issues.

Why Do Kids Use?

People seek drugs and alcohol to ease their pain for a variety of reasons, but addiction is often caused by early childhood stress and trauma. We know that children who have a stressful or traumatic early life experience have a greater chance of substance use. Early childhood neglect or abuse can lead a child to turn to substances to numb their pain and unexpressed feelings. Childhood trauma of any kind causes stress for adolescents and can be what motivates them to look for an escape from their feelings.

Divorce, illness, death, abuse, financial stress, and mental illness are some of the additional issues kids and families face. Genetics can also play a role. Your child may have trouble making friends. A father or mother may no longer be in their child's life, for various reasons, and this can be painful. Occasionally, a parent is coping with his or her own substance use problem, which of course causes problems for the child.

While trauma can be the root cause of substance use, it can be complex, and experiences can affect people differently. The Kaiser Adverse Childhood Experiences (ACEs) study showed that childhood experiences significantly impact a person's ability to achieve lifelong health and opportunities. The study also revealed that childhood trauma could increase the risk of early substance use.

When kids first start down the road of experimentation, they may not understand what they are feeling. They may be just trying to fit in with their peers. Then there are the kids who, because of their brain chemistry, environment, or the stressors in their life, find that the use of drugs and alcohol numbs their pain and allows them to escape whatever discomfort they are feeling. Substances solve a problem for them, and it works for a while. Use may later escalate to where drinking or smoking marijuana becomes a daily habit, and from there to even more problematic drug use. Too many parents find themselves, ten years later, still trying to cope with their child's problem.

It is always healthier for kids to be drug-free during the teen years, because their brains are still developing. Some parents get a pass and their kids never show any interest in alcohol or drug use—perhaps because of their upbringing, or because they're not interested in the risk-taking involved with substance use. They may have found other activities that they enjoy, so they don't feel the need to turn to drugs.

For others, experimentation can be a short-lived activity that burns out early on. Some teens use drugs or alcohol moderately during their high school years but can continue to manage their use and don't move on to harder drugs. Some teens or young adults are binge users who engage in drug or alcohol use for a while, then stop for a while, then start again. Substances affect people in different ways, which makes the problem complicated and confusing.

A word of caution about opioid use after surgery for pain. Doctors are more aware of the problem now and it seems that efforts to screen for dependence before prescribing are being made. But over-prescribing still happens, so as a parent, it is important to be an advocate for your child and to closely monitor any prescriptions that they are given. Too many teens and young adults have become dependent because of an opioid prescription they were given by a doctor for an injury and parents assumed it was safe. And the ease of getting pills of any kind is obviously a big issue with teens.

Behavioral Issues

Like any disease, substance use also has typical symptoms, such as hostile behavior, including lying and stealing, and legal issues. Being honest is challenging for someone with a substance use issue, who is usually hiding their use from parents and other family members. Yet most were probably honest individuals before they started using drugs. Parents want to believe their children, but trying to outguess them becomes tiring. We can grow resentful as it quickly becomes a game of cat and mouse.

Stealing to be able to buy more drugs is also a common issue. One mom wrote, "She has done so many things to us and this home that I can't trust her with anything. I also can't let her live on the street, so I'm like a prisoner in my own home." Families have lost jewelry and precious family heirlooms.

Legal issues are another problem that families face. One mom shared how her son broke into their neighbor's home to steal, which was embarrassing and heartbreaking as well as illegal. Jail is not a pleasant thought for any parent. For some, it can be a turning point. The idea of having a child with legal issues causes a great deal of stress for parents. As one mom explained it, "The thought that my daughter is going through this and I can't do anything to stop it has affected my life in every way."

Parents also feel judged when sharing the news with family and friends. Well-meaning family members may offer advice that is not always helpful. This can result in isolation, as parents feel alone with the shame and stigma—no one wants to be judged as a bad parent. Grandparents can be affected, too; they are often baffled about why their grandchild is having so many problems. Sometimes grandparents and other family members can give unsolicited advice, which leads to more stress and pain.

Parents may make attempts to compartmentalize their feelings so that they can function at work. They may limit their social interactions with friends and family. It feels awkward to have to answer questions about how your son or daughter is doing, especially when you hear how well your friend's children are doing.

Disciplining your way out of this problem rarely works either. Instead, it causes shutting down, confrontation, arguing, and resistance. The reality is that parents are not trained on how to deal with their child's use. Understandably, they are often left grasping for answers, and wondering what will happen next. Will their child use drugs again? Will this be the time he overdoses? When will they get the call? This continual worry can lead a parent to depression and anxiety.

Getting Help

Even if your child does agree to go to treatment, a program may be financially out of reach. Some have borrowed money, used college funds, or taken out a second mortgage on their home.

Too many people do not have available support services. Parents may find themselves calling helplines, friends, family, and even strangers looking for answers on what to do next. They may have to wait weeks for a bed to open up through a state or county-funded program, often calling the treatment program every day to see if one is available. This can prove frustrating for someone attempting to make changes in their life, who needs help now.

Getting Tough

If efforts to help their child change do not pay off, it may have an emotional, mental, and physical effect on parents. In cases like this, parents are sometimes at a crossroads, unsure what to do next when their child is unwilling to get help. They feel they have given all the necessary support they can, yet there is no visible change.

They ask themselves; *Do I use tough love? Kick him out? Let him stay? Or continue to offer love and support?* They want to know when to push and when to step back.

When I went through this with my child, I heard many different messages. I longed for a roadmap so that I had some direction. It adds to the stress when you don't know which path to follow.

I remember going to the family weekend at my daughter's treatment program. The counselor gave us a final direction not to allow our daughter in the house if she relapsed. While I nodded and said *"Okay,"* but in my heart, I couldn't imagine closing the door on one of my children.

Some parents look to tough love for the answer. One of the problems with tough love is that people have different definitions of what it means. Some view it as a way to wake their kid up and let them know there will be zero tolerance for the negative behavior.

Yet, a harsh disciplinary approach can cause harm by pushing a teen or young adult further into their substance use and more resistant to change. It may damage, possibly even permanently, your relationship with your child. The tough-love process can cause more harm to an already traumatized young person.

Too often, the advice we hear is to let our child hit "rock bottom." "Just detach." "Let them figure it out." "They have to want it."

or "Why are you wasting your time?" But then who is going to help our child who is suffering?

Try a Proven Positive Approach

According to Elizabeth Hartney, PhD, "While tough love can sometimes force people with substance and alcohol use disorders into treatment, research suggests that more empathetic, voluntary approaches are more effective. For example, studies have shown that a program known as Community Reinforcement and Family Training (CRAFT) can help people encourage their loved ones to seek treatment. The program utilizes behavioral principles to reduce substance use, encourage treatment, and reduce the stress felt by the individual's loved ones."

The sooner you are proactive in the addiction process and encourage your child to get help, the greater the chances they will bypass the continued negative consequences of continual dependence. Every time you encourage your child, it can bring them closer to be willing to change their life.

Substance use is a complex problem for families. While it can seem overwhelming, there are tools that can get results by addressing the situation in a more compassionate way. Some of these strategies you may already be doing intuitively, and others will be helpful to learn as you work through the problem.

What I have learned is that compassion also works to strengthen, rather than weaken, your relationship with your child. The stronger your relationship, the greater the likelihood that your child will listen to you and be willing to make some changes. As I've worked with parents who begin to change the way they engage with their child, it's rewarding to see things start to improve. As one mom said, "I changed the way I talked to my son, and things started to change for the better."

Case Study: Susan, Jason, and Charlie

Susan and Jason reached out to me a few years ago about their son Charlie. The family lived in a suburb in Kansas. Susan and Jason had adopted Charlie and his sister Kaitlyn as newborns. Then after several years, Susan became pregnant with her son, Daniel. Charlie had struggled with a learning disability which wasn't discovered until high school.

Through the years, school had been a challenge for Charlie. He had graduated from high school and was attending a local junior college where he had done well. He applied to several four-year colleges and was excited to be accepted to his top pick in Chicago.

He attended the college in the fall as a transfer student and decided to join a fraternity. From what Susan and Jason could tell, things seemed to be going well. Charlie had met new friends and liked his classes. Charlie came home for Christmas break and seemed to be doing fine, yet Susan had a feeling that things were stressful for Charlie. After going back in January, things seemed to be more difficult for Charlie during his second semester,

In March, Susan and Jason got a call from Charlie that he needed help. He was having trouble with academics and told his parents he had failed two of his classes from the first semester. The fraternity wasn't working for him, and he needed to leave school.

Charlie wanted to come home and thought he had a problem. He finally admitted that he had been drinking heavily at college. Susan and Jason were disappointed after Charlie had put so much effort in applying to the four-year college. It turned out that he had blacked out twice at a couple frat parties and knew he had embarrassed himself at a few others. Charlie wanted to come home and spend time during the spring to get his drinking under control. He hoped he could go back to college the following fall semester. He told his parents he had been drinking every day at that point.

Charlie felt embarrassed and that he had let his family down. Charlie's sister, Kaitlyn, who was two years younger, had done well in school, was on the soccer and swim teams, and excelled both in her academics and sports. They had been close at one point, but Kaitlyn was frustrated about all of Charlie's issues in high school and now college. Charlie felt he wasn't a role model for his younger brother, Daniel, and felt bad about that.

Charlie came home and was depressed. He felt terrible about what had happened at school. His friends that lived near his home all drank. Rather than get together with them and start drinking again, he stayed home and spent long hours alone in his room.

Susan wanted her son to be able to drink socially, yet she wasn't sure how to help him keep his drinking under control. She felt drinking was everywhere, and it would be easier if Charlie could drink alcohol moderately.

Charlie agreed to attend an intensive outpatient program (IOP) at the local hospital and see a therapist.

Jason and Susan wanted to be supportive and help their son. Yet at the same time, Susan, particularly, felt the urge to want to fix him and was running out of patience with the problem. They decided to go to an Al-Anon meeting and found it helpful, but they also wanted to know how to talk to their son, so things stayed positive. They wanted to stay close to him and wanted him to live at home for the time being.

Susan was worried she hadn't done the right things raising Charlie. Yet they had provided a tutor for Charlie to help with his learning disability. They had paid for a counselor on and off for several years as well. She had worked part-time but had been available to her kids while they were growing up. Susan clearly loved her son, but felt scared and alone. She wanted to be strong but felt this was a difficult time for her. Jason was more relaxed about the problem. He had many responsibilities at work but also wanted to do whatever he could to help Charlie.

After attending the IOP and working with his counselor, Charlie decided to stop drinking. Susan is supportive of her son but also had mixed feelings. A part of her is embarrassed and doesn't want to have to explain to people why her son isn't drinking. But she is committed to working on herself and supporting Charlie, as is Jason. Charlie decided to take a year off and then make a decision about going back to college. He has since had a slip but is continuing to work on himself and stay sober.

Chapter Summary

- Addiction doesn't discriminate and affects people from all walks of life.
- Most drug or alcohol dependence starts in the teen years.
- Parents can second-guess themselves and struggle for years with stress, anxiety, and fear. Yet most parents are doing the best they can with a difficult problem.
- There are many risk factors that can lead to addiction, including trauma, genetics, early use, mental health issues, impulsiveness, and environment.
- The shame and stigma around addiction gets in the way of parents and other family members seeking help.
- Compassion can strengthen your relationship with your child.

PART 2:
COMPASSION

CHAPTER 3

A Compassionate Approach

In term of addictions, first of all recognize that these people are traumatized and what they need is not more trauma and punishment but more compassion. —*Dr. Gabor Maté*

One of my favorite tenets of CRAFT is the idea of creating a life that competes with substances. —*Jill P.*

Have you been irritated and annoyed at your child's situation? Have you watched that irritation spread throughout your family as the problem dragged on and grew more serious? Would you feel differently about your child's substance problem if you knew why it was happening and were aware of your child's underlying pain and suffering?

Compassion can be the most valuable tool when it comes to addiction. For parents, having a clear understanding of why your kids have chosen to use drugs or alcohol and what you can do to help them change is critical. We parents *can* learn to help and influence our kids during this difficult time.

Many young people seem to be functioning well. Yet inside, they feel distressed and trapped. Drugs and alcohol are a tempting escape. Using substances can soothe the pain, or at least distract from it.

Taking the time to have compassion for what your child is going through can help. Discovering the underlying issues by getting to the root of the problem can be what will lead your child to getting back on track.

Why?

Substance use is not something our kids do *to* us, as their parents. Instead, it is a form of escape from the intense discomfort in themselves and their world.

One mom wrote about how her son has been misusing alcohol and drugs to cope with depression and anxiety for over ten years. "He is twenty-seven. It has been a very tough situation for our family, and I'm his only support."

Another mom wrote that her daughter has underlying depression and anxiety issues. "I'm a chronic anxiety sufferer, so I understand her flare-ups entirely. I'm concerned she will relapse because of them. For these last few months, she's admitted to doing just about everything over the past 12 years. She didn't show signs of drug use. Even after she moved after college, her apartment was always clean, she held a full-time job, showed up for family things, never looked sick or strung out. But she ran short of money all the time. It wasn't until that last month before last July that we questioned why she couldn't make rent. And then, a few weeks later, the call came that changed our lives."

A third wrote that her oldest son, who is seventeen, has been struggling with marijuana use for about three years. "He was adopted as a baby. His mother had a drug addiction before her pregnancy with him. His adoptive father and I are now divorced. He is a senior in high school and struggles with marijuana use, despite the problematic consequences. He admits that he has a hard time stopping and says he begs his friends to give it to him. He indicates he is depressed at times. He has seen three different counselors, two of which were addiction specialists, to no avail."

The question almost every parent asks themselves when they realize their child has turned to substance use is *"Why?"* Once you know the cause, you can then help your child. So often, the answer to the substance use problem lies in our child's lives and experiences.

How Compassion Creates Positive Change

Compassion is helpful in any situation, so of course it's also beneficial for someone struggling with substance use. People can change for the better. While it's not always easy, as parents we can be more compassionate and encourage change to happen.

We can retrain ourselves in how we think of substance use and addiction. Rather than viewing it as a moral failing, we can treat the affliction with the urgency and compassion we do other chronic illnesses.

Studies conducted by Dr. Robert J. Meyers and his colleagues at the University of New Mexico have shown that family members of a person misusing drugs or alcohol can reduce stress and regain control of their lives while making treatment options more attractive. His CRAFT approach is less punitive and more compassionate and has been shown to reduce substance use and increase the chances that a person will agree to seek help.

The studies done with adolescents come out the same as adult studies, with an average of 70 percent engagement. Concerned

Significant Others (CSOs), which include parents, partners, spouses, or siblings, have the same success in getting the patient into treatment.

CRAFT has three goals:

1. To teach you skills to take care of yourself.
2. To teach you skills you can use to help your loved one change.
3. To reduce substance use, period, whether your loved one gets formal treatment or not.

Jeff Foote, PhD, director of the Center for Motivation and Change and the CMC: Foundation for Change, says, "We know many specific things DO help in this very complicated and often terrifying process, and it is important to me to get the word out… to give families who are trying so hard some needed and reality-based hope."

Traditional approaches with family members and treatment programs don't consider what life experiences have motivated a person to start down the road to addiction. Negative consequences such as living on the street, not getting enough food or sleep, or being locked up because of substance use don't often lead to positive change. People are already traumatized—that is why they have chosen to use drugs or alcohol. Punishing your child for their substance use is unlikely to motivate them to change.

Fill Your Own Cup First

For us to feel compassion for our children, we can't be running on empty. Feeling stressed or overwhelmed blocks us from developing an understanding of ourselves and our children. When we're stressed out, we aren't calm or peaceful. We feel insecure, we distance ourselves from others, and we may lack the capacity for joy.

Substance use disorders affect your child—and in addition, other family members feel the negative impact of the problem. You may have problems arise due to your child's substance use, including financial, health, work productivity, and relationship issues. You may also experience more stress and depression and feel overall less happy about your life. It's hard to stay focused and balanced when you are continually worried about your child.

Substance use is a painful problem. While it's natural to want the pain to go away—especially since substance use can take a while to correct itself—know that you *can* help your child while also feeling pain at the same time. When you do things to support yourself and stay resilient, you will feel less overwhelmed. Later in the book, I'll go into more detail about self-care.

What I have found when working with parents is that as they changed the way the approached the problem, their children started to be more open, less defensive, and less confrontational. Changing the conversation can be transformational not only to your child but to you as well. It starts with self-care and self-awareness. It may seem like a small tweak, yet when you come at the problem with understanding and compassion, it can lead to a big change.

Often people in recovery report that family influenced their decision to enter treatment or to get some other kind of help. You, as a parent, can encourage your child to live a healthier lifestyle. You can motivate your child to let go of or lessen their use of drugs or alcohol.

Parents of substance users are stressed, anxious, and filled with fear, often because of the chaos they are experiencing. The strategies in the CRAFT approach are the opposite of drama. The lack of drama is what can change your families' lives for the better.

There is no quick fix when it comes to substance use. You may not get it right the first time. Yet it is worth it to keep trying. Look for those windows of opportunity. You will feel better and see a positive difference in your loved one. CRAFT gives parents and families tools that they can use themselves. It helps communication within the family and makes for a better future for all involved.

Then Fill Their Cup

If you decide to change your approach and attempt to be more compassionate with your child, it's important to know that you may not see immediate results. Change takes time and patience. But as a parent, you will most likely feel less depressed and anxious and as a result your child will feel better about themselves.

I've learned that with a compassionate approach, the chances are better that your child will be willing to change their lifestyle. There will be less suffering, even if you are not able to motivate your child to enter treatment. I can't tell you the number of moms I've talked to who have been relieved when they realized they could approach their child's problem with more kindness and compassion.

When it comes to compassion and substance use, some may feel that we're giving our kids a pass on their negative behavior. But being more compassionate does not mean you are not holding them accountable.

Being willing to get help and change their life is your child's responsibility, once they realize and accept that they have a substance use problem. They need to manage their life, stay healthy, and learn not to impact family members and friends. You can't do this work for them. All of this is still true, whether you look on the situation with compassion or don't.

Taking responsibility for your part is essential. Watching your child suffer and wondering what to do next is both painful and fruitless. If you can take on some of that suffering, transform it into a more positive message, and offer that to your child, it could help promote their recovery. Shining a light on addiction, talking about it openly, and treating your struggling child with more compassion and positive support *will help.* It may be what your child needs to have the strength to move forward and have hope for a better tomorrow.

Chris Grosso is the author of *Dead Set on Living: Making the Difficult but Beautiful Journey from F#*king Up to Waking Up.* In his recovery from drugs and alcohol, Chris wrote his popular book to better understand why he continued to relapse, why other people continue to turn to self-defeating behaviors, and how they can recover, heal, and thrive. He interviewed luminaries and best-selling authors to help him find the answers. One of the authors is Dr. Gabor Maté, who sums up in the most beautiful way how parents can cope with a child's substance use. Chris says:

"I wanted to know about family members who are dealing with addiction. What can they do for a loved one who's caught in the grips of active addiction? Because when people are that deep in addiction, they've lost themselves—they're gone in a way. I know I was. I know there was nothing my family could have done no matter how much they wanted to."

Gabor didn't agree with Chris. "Imagine if your family had come and said, 'Chris, here's how it is. We recognize that your addiction is not your primary problem. Your primary problem is that you're in a lot of pain. And that pain is not yours alone. That pain has been carried in our family for generations. And we're as much a part of that pain as you are. You're just the one who's soothing it with that behavior. In fact, you're the one whose behavior shows us how much pain there is in our family. Thank you for showing that to us.'"

Gabor went on to say, "We're going to take on the task of healing ourselves. We invite you to be there if you feel like it. And if you're not ready, sweetheart, then just do what you need to do right now."

Shame Gets in the Way

Addiction and shame go hand in hand—so much so that it's hard to understand where one starts and the other ends. When our kids are struggling, we can be left feeling powerless, isolated, and unworthy. There is a strong sense of secrecy and silence around substance use disorder. It can feel easier to hide and not talk about it. Shame gets in the way of having compassion for yourself and your child.

You may feel as if you are a bad parent and somehow deserve this—so you try to hide the problem. You don't want people to know the truth. The emotional burden that parents take on affects all of the other aspects of their health and well-being. So what can you do about this? A lot. But it's a process, not a one-time event!

According to Adi Jaffe, PhD, author of *The Abstinence Myth: A New Approach for Overcoming Addiction Without Shame, Judgment, or Rules,* "Shame is the feeling that there's something wrong with you. It's not about having done something wrong (that's guilt); no, shame arises from the core belief that you are simply not good enough. Sadly, it's a core belief that is common among those who struggle with addiction issues."

We all feel shame at some point in our lives, sometimes at a very early age. Family influence plays a significant role in how a child views himself. A child who feels shame may start to act out or shut down as shame becomes part of their nature. If a child is repeatedly humiliated by someone they look up to, it can lead to a lifetime of struggle.

And shame can isolate you. It can hold you back from reaching out for help. Some believe they can handle the problem themselves, preferring to keep their troubles and embarrassment behind closed doors. It's heartbreaking to hear from a parent who has not reached out for support because of the shame and stigma of addiction.

But if we recognize our shame, we can begin to learn how to turn it around. If you find yourself looking back with regrets, remember that there is no training manual for dealing with a child struggling with substances. Remind yourself that most parents do their best to raise their children in a loving home. Loving parents who have tried to do all the right things can still raise a child who struggles with drugs or alcohol, just as well-adjusted kids can come from families who struggle with many problems.

Many parents don't know what to do, so they hope that the problem will correct itself. In the beginning, I felt that way too. As parents, we may go into denial rather than face the challenging issues surrounding our child's problem. But when we avoid the problem, our stress level rises, and our child will continue to suffer because it takes longer for him or her to receive help.

You've lost the dream you had for your child. You see the harm being done. Understandably, you are thinking about what you could have done differently. While it is essential to acknowledge the past, please don't dwell on it. Instead, learn from your mistakes. Use those lessons as tools for a better tomorrow. Your history does not have to shape your future.

Accept the situation for what it is, as complicated as it may be, and start looking for support. When you can accept the problem, you'll have a better chance of finding peace in your life and not dwelling on what could have been. We know there are no guarantees in life. Even if the situation doesn't change right away, your acceptance will help you cope in a healthier way.

Staying isolated is what allows shame to grow and magnify. The simple act of talking about your child's use will shine a light on the problem and bring it out of the shadows. It will be easier to forgive yourself as you realize how many others are in a similar situation. Self-compassion will begin to come more easily to you, eradicating the shame as it does. Remind your child, too, even if they are an adult, that they are essentially good people, but their action is not acceptable or appropriate. That approach gives a person a healthier outlook.

Connecting with Others

When we reach out to others, it can help alleviate the shame around substance use. It takes courage to tell our addiction story and all that we have gone through with others. And when we do, it brings us closer to letting go of our shame and reconnecting.

Through our connections with others who are walking the same path, we can find healing. We can support each other and learn from each other's experiences. We develop a support network. We gain power and feel better about ourselves.

Family members who are affected by a loved one's substance use may believe it is up to them to keep the family running despite the problem, which itself may be as harmful as the original problem of addiction. Look to trusted family and friends to support you during this time. Steer away from people who make you feel judged. You don't need harsh criticism in your life right now.

Too often, parents believe that they can handle the problem themselves, and prefer to keep their troubles behind closed doors. But shame can grow when you don't reach out for help. The simple act of talking about your child's substance use will shine a light on the problem and bring it out of the shadows. Find people you can trust to share the pain with, and/or find a professional that can help you.

We also reduce our feelings of shame when we listen to other people with compassion. We don't have to be born compassionate—it is something we can learn. We can feel compassion for someone else's story, and listening helps us accept our own story with all its flaws. Compassion is not about healing the other person; compassion is about two people listening to each other and feeling better about what is going on in their lives. Understanding and loving others is a commitment we can make when we are willing to practice listening and understanding another person's painful stories.

Have compassion for yourself as well. What would you tell a friend who is buckling under the pressure and strain of a child's drug use issues? When you permit yourself to let go of all the guilt, shame, and what-ifs, regrets fade away. You can focus on more helpful, positive things.

Forgiveness

See if you can forgive yourself for your past mistakes. Learn from them, of course, but treat yourself gently. Being able to accept and forgive yourself is vital. It helps your child do the same. When you practice self-compassion, you are being a role model for your child struggling with addiction. You remind them that they are a cherished and valuable person.

With self-compassion comes forgiveness. We can forgive others who we feel have wronged us. We can also forgive ourselves for any missteps in the past. The research of Fred Luskin, PhD, author and Director of the Stanford Forgiveness Projects, showed that "Learning to forgive helps people hurt less, experience less anger, feel less stress, and suffer less depression. As people learn to forgive, they become more hopeful, optimistic and compassionate."

Forgiveness is an essential part of the healing process. While it is important to forgive our loved ones, it is also important to forgive ourselves. When we forgive, we set ourselves free.

You can find ways to be less affected by the shame of addiction when you reach out for support, and support groups have helped many. Sometimes issues are critical, and you need individual help. Sometimes having one-on-one help goes a lot further in a shorter amount of time than waiting for your turn to talk in a group. Think about what works best for you.

I have found that knowing someone who has gone through a similar experience helps me to feel lighter and more hopeful. But I didn't know where to turn when I first realized substance use was a problem in my family. I told some friends, and lucky for me, the response was supportive.

One friend in particular was a good resource. Her child had gone to treatment programs, so she knew how stressful substance use could be. She offered to go to a support group meeting with me. It made all the difference to have someone lead the way and help me to get started with support. Many parents I've worked with have found community support through counselors, coaches, groups, friends, or family. Find what works for you.

Case Study: Diane, Rich and David

Diane reached out to me, explaining that her adult son David was living at home because he had struggled with a drug problem for years. Diane and her husband, Rich, had tried their best to get David some help.

The problem went from bad to worse. David tried to cover up his drug use and told his parents that he had it under control and could stop at any time.

Diane explained,

"When we would discover that David had stolen something from us or found his stash, I knew Rich was going to get angry. Unfortunately he yelled at David and called him names. He threatened to kick him out, which we had done before, but we backed down when David became emotional and begged us to let him stay.

"The yelling, arguing, and threats seemed like a weekly occurrence, yet David could not stop using substances. I would make Rich sit with me, and we would review ideas from the books I had read and write out what would be said. We had to learn not to react quickly because that always led to an ugly argument.

"We did give David ultimatums. Some worked, and some didn't. We went through six rounds of different detox programs and rehabs. It took that long for David to be ready to embrace recovery finally.

"We are finally feeling a little bit of peace. I have regrets about how we reacted, but through this experience, I've learned patience.

"Recovery is not always an easy road. My son has been sober for nine months. At times, he can still seem unhappy, which is hard to watch. I know it's tough to be still living at home. Rich and I sometimes have to leave the house so that we don't lose it. I thought he would get happier right away, but that hasn't been the case. Yet, it is getting better, and we are starting to see his former self come through more often.

"And for the first time in seven years, I'm not dreading the holidays. It is amazing! There was a time when Rich and I were discussing how we would handle David's funeral.

"I prayed every day for David to have courage. He had to face drug court to untangle his legal issues, which saved his life and mine. We were at a point where we were okay with whatever it took. We just wanted our boy back.

"Have faith that your child will find his way. Relax from time to time and be thankful your child is still alive. Know that it takes time. You never know what tomorrow will bring."

Chapter Summary

- Compassion can be a valuable tool for working with addiction.
- As a parent, you can learn to help your child and guide them toward change.
- Punishing your child for their substance use is unlikely to motivate them to change.
- CRAFT gives parents and families tools that they can use themselves.
- Shame can isolate you. It can hold you back from reaching out for help.
- Connect with others and have compassion for yourself.

CHAPTER 4

Taking Care of Ourselves

If you are unable to take care of yourself, how can you take care of anyone else? How can you take care of the person you love? When you are here for yourself, when you have reestablished some basic order and peace within yourself, then you can take care of your son, your daughter, your partner, or your friend. But if you are not able to be here for yourself, it will not be possible for you to be here for them. That's why you must come back to yourself.
—Thich Nhat Hanh

Walking has always made me feel better, mind, body, spirit. Some days I have to make myself, but the benefit is worth it!
—Kay W.

As you deal with the constant stress of your child's substance use, do you feel like you're being sucked deeper and deeper into a vortex, with no way out? If so, you're not alone. When we're dealing with substance use, taking care of ourselves needs to be a priority. This is something that is easy to lose sight of when we are concerned about our child, so I appreciate that CRAFT emphasizes self-care.

Some equate self-care with selfishness, yet it's one of the kindest things we can do for those we love. It increases our ability to support them, and to model what self-care looks like so they can do the same. If you don't care for yourself, you may end up needing someone to take care of *you*.

Helping your child starts with loving yourself. Yet self-care is a step that I often see as a last priority. You may feel that you need to put all your effort into helping your struggling child. That is understandable.

It's easy, especially for mothers with a son or daughter struggling with drug or alcohol use, to end up running on empty. If we neglect self-care, we pay the price. When we deplete our inner resources, we have nothing left to give.

And keep in mind that you are a role model for your child—and when you practice self-care, your son or daughter will see you living a healthy life. Make it a priority to fill up your tank! I have found that if I take care of myself regularly, I am a better parent, friend, and support person for everyone in my life. You'll be more helpful to your child during the recovery process if you take care of yourself first.

Our kids need our strength. They need us to make logical decisions, based not on fear but on supporting long-term change. As you begin helping your child through their substance use issues, it is easy to get entangled in their problems and not be aware of where your emotions end and theirs begin. It can feel like you are both drowning together.

The answer to this problem is to care for yourself, the caregiver, with compassion. When you do, you will feel more equipped to deal with situations as they come up. There are many ways to support yourself, as we will get into later in the book. The more you do, the more emotionally stable you will be, and the better shape you'll be in to keep supporting your child.

As long as your child is on this journey, so are you. You need to be capable of facing these issues over the long haul, if it comes to that. If you exhaust yourself in the process, you will have lost yourself as well as your child.

Self-Awareness

I urge you to let this period take you on a conscious journey of self-discovery, personal growth, and self-development. Parents who prioritize this come away better off than they were before any trouble started!

I wanted to understand what my children were going through, and gaining a better understanding of myself helped me so much with this. A combination of asking for outside support, journal writing, yoga, meditation, and exercise helped. At times I would slip back into my old ways. But I learned how much better I felt when I was taking care of myself, and that good feeling helped motivate me.

Be aware of your physical, emotional, and mental health. Nurture yourself. You may face some fallout from the situation with your child, and you need the inner strength to fight those battles too.

Lay your foundation of self-care. It will take time and effort on your part—but it will be worth it. Taking care of yourself will give you the resilience you will need in the days, weeks, months, and years ahead.

Discovering your child is struggling with substances is one of the most challenging things you will go through. But it can also be a golden opportunity to better understand what led your family to this place.

During my children's middle and high school years, I was teaching full-time as a single mom. Even though their dad was involved on a regular basis, I felt like I was treading water to stay afloat, and it was all I could do just to get through each day.

When I discovered that my children were struggling with substance use, it was a turning point in my life. I realized how programmed my life had been. My commitments had been running me, rather than me taking charge of my own life. I had lost touch with myself.

I knew things needed to change, so I decided I needed to carve out some time for myself. I felt like I had been marching through life in a trance, one foot in front of the other. I needed time to think about how I wanted to change my life going forward, and I wanted things to be different for myself and my children. I wanted to gain something positive from all the pain that I was feeling.

Choose Not to Suffer Alone

When I discovered that my kids had issues with substance use, my reaction was to hide out, stay in the house, keep it a secret, and pretend it wasn't happening. The last thing I wanted to do was to share my family's problems with friends or extended family. Yet, as time went on, I knew I needed to continue to help myself stay strong.

As embarrassed as I was, I reached out to friends who I thought could help. From each person, I got a little something that helped me feel better. One took me to a meeting. Another gave me the name of a counselor who could help us find a treatment program. Others just listened and were supportive.

I also got help by reaching out for counseling, practicing yoga on a more regular basis, and starting to run several times a week. Running helped get my adrenaline going. Adding a few extra supports into my life gave me the strength to go on—in my own life and work and to help my family heal.

But I can't say it enough: what worked for me isn't necessarily what will work for you. You may need to *remove* a few things from your life—that may be the kindest, most supportive path for you. You may need to try a few things and see what helps.

Addressing your emotional, social, physical, and spiritual health will help you stay grounded. You'll be less likely to fall into the giant pit of fatigue and feel like giving up.

Emotional Well-Being

It's common knowledge that emotional health includes:

- Resilience in hard times
- Consistent self-care
- Self-awareness
- Positive relationships
- Self-acceptance
- The ability to manage feelings
- A sense of optimism and wellness

When one person in the family is struggling, everyone in the family is affected. Parents in particular suffer deeply when their kids are struggling, and many go through a myriad of emotions. Although it is different for everyone, guilt, grief, and shame are often present.

Many parents I've talked to will feel guilty for not having known earlier. They may wish they had been able to stop or prevent the addiction and may even feel that it was their fault somehow. Parents may stew over what they might have done in the past that caused what is happening now, and wonder what they could have done to make it all turn out differently. These intense feelings can be unbearable.

Then there is often a grieving process that parents go through, having lost their hopes and dreams for their child. Aspirations parents hold for the kids seem to disappear before their eyes.

This form of grief is real. Sadness accompanies any loss. With addiction, those losses are broad and deep. Processing grief varies in duration for everyone. It can be quick, or it can take years.

While it's not always easy, you must make a conscious effort to feel the pain and loss, so it can pass and you can move on.

You may feel, at times, as though your emotional state is a direct reflection of how well your child is doing. It is a troublesome path when your well-being is dictated by a situation that feels out of control. This is not a good position to be in! It's been said that recovery is a marathon, not a sprint, so think about developing sustainability—a way to stay resilient. Think about how you can help yourself stay afloat.

To help our children, we need to help ourselves first. It may be hard to believe this now, but you can find happiness even when your child is struggling. Working through their substance use can be a turning point for the whole family—a wake-up call that gives all family members the chance to recognize how they can do better and become the best versions of themselves.

Social Well-Being

People are meant to live and thrive in a community. As parents of young adults and troubled kids, we often let go of our social connections and shy away, isolate, or otherwise lose the social network that we had. Our social well-being may be compromised when our children struggle.

The situation may cause distance from those who can best support us at this critical time. The stigma can envelop us. Addiction is still too often seen in a criminal light. This approach makes the problems worse because people aren't getting the help that they need. Certainly, some people who have encountered legal issues have used that experience to change their life. Yet we've seen through the years that this isn't necessarily an effective or compassionate approach when the root of the problem is a mental health issue. And while we are making progress, in general, the criminal justice system does not deal with addiction in an equal and fair way. Basic services need to be provided so that they are easily accessible. In his book *American Fix: Inside the Opioid Addiction Crisis—And How to End It,* Ryan Hampton states, "Incarceration without recovery programming is ineffective for people who are coping with addiction. It's common sense: Isolation and punishing doesn't work. Love, inclusion, and help *do.*"

Whether your child has legal issues or not, you and your family may be treated differently by friends and family who assume the worst about the situation. Sometimes this is subtle, and sometimes it is not. One parent was left out of neighborhood parties after being a part of them for years. Friends and family may back away from you because they are uncomfortable with your situation. They may want to give you suggestions on what to do. Younger siblings can find themselves suddenly not invited to playdates. These kinds of things are hurtful, but they happen.

Your child may also feel isolated and shunned if their friends, school, or place of employment discover that they are or were misusing substances. I've talked to a number of moms whose children have come home after a treatment program to find themselves spending most of their time alone. This is in part because their friends are still using, but also because people are keeping their distance. One mom shared how her two daughters really didn't want to have much to do with their sister who had been struggling on and off with alcohol, which put her in the middle. Social well-being is important for you and your family. It's crucial to feeling good about yourself.

In short, having a troubled child or young adult can and often does strain relationships in one way or another. People don't always know what to say—so often, they will say nothing, or ask painful questions. It's easy to feel alone.

What to Do

How, then, do you take care of your social well-being? First, be conscious and aware of what is happening to you socially. Make a concerted effort to get what you need in this area of your life.

This looks different for everyone. Consider reaching out to others you know who are going through something similar. Support groups can be helpful for some. Reach out to family and friends you trust, to get together socially or have someone to talk with about what you are going through. Life doesn't stop, even when we're in crisis—and especially when the crisis is long-lasting, as addiction can be.

You can pick up an old hobby and benefit from the social interaction it brings. Volunteer work can help you think about something else for a while, if that makes sense for you. You can use this time to strengthen family relationships, to have people in your life who are close to you.

Think about how you can shore up your social life. You are the only one with the answers, and you are the only one who can make it happen. Your social well-being matters now more than ever.

Physical Well-Being

Survival mode means we are getting through each day—just putting one foot in front of the other, mentally and emotionally drained. Addiction can do that to all of us. You can become burnt out when trying to deal with your child's substance use problems.

We need water, food, sunlight, fresh air, and movement for our physical well-being. When we get wrapped up in survival mode, we often lose sight of these basic requirements.

Ask Yourself

How am I doing *now*? (Not before the crisis hit.)

Am I getting 6–8 hours of sleep a night?

Am I eating fresh, healthy food?

Am I drinking enough water?

Am I scheduling regular dentist and doctor appointments?

Do I wear sunscreen?

Do I know enough about my health and what my body needs?

How often do I exercise? Is it enjoyable and fun?

These questions are not intended to make you feel bad or guilty—but simply to assess how well you are taking care of yourself right now. Remember, your child's situation can go on for months or years, but you can't ignore your health for that long!

Regular physical exercise can calm your mind, keep you focused, and help you make better decisions. Moving the body improves our mood, relieves stress, and stimulates brain chemicals that leave us feeling healthier and more relaxed. Try to engage in some physical activity and see how you feel when you do.

You'll also likely sleep better after you exercise. If you have experienced sleepless nights due to worry, you know that everything is harder when you're tired. Regular physical activity can help you fall asleep faster and deepen your sleep. If you don't push your body during the day, you may sleep more lightly and it may be hard to fall into the deep sleep that you need.

How much exercise do you need to take advantage of these benefits? Getting outside for a 30-minute walk every day is fantastic. Do you have a partner or friend who might enjoy a walk? Take him or her with you. Do you have a dog? He or she will probably be thrilled if they get to go out with you. A child might go with you too—the struggling one, one of your other children, or both. Walks are a wonderful way to enjoy some one-on-one time together. Getting outside of your own four walls changes your perspective and makes everything seem more manageable.

Yoga and running can be helpful as well, to ease your mind and help tone your body. See what classes your local gym offers and pick one that sounds like fun. And you might want to try mixing it up, so you don't get bored.

Setting aside time each day for movement helps to form a habit. Are you more likely to exercise in the morning, lunchtime, or evening? Find the time that works best for you and jot it down on your calendar, and you'll be more likely to follow through. Perhaps send yourself an email or text reminder, so you don't forget.

I've found that it helps to start small. At first I would run for a block or two, and then I extended the distance. If you simply take a walk around the block for a few minutes a day, it won't seem overwhelming. Every few days, you can increase your distance or time, to what feels doable. Remember—if it's fun, you'll look forward to doing it, so pick something you'll enjoy. I like to listen to music or a podcast when I walk, which gives me something to focus on.

Another thing that I've found helpful is to lay out my workout clothes, shoes, and other gear the night before. I found myself more likely to get out the door if I could see everything I needed, especially if it was early in the morning. Also, having an accountability partner can be helpful. When a friend is counting on me to show up, I'm more likely to do it.

When you exercise, you're focusing on that moment in time, which allows your mind to take a break from the constant worrying. On the other hand, it can be a time when ideas and solutions come to mind.

When you take care of your physical body, you're in a better position to support your child's long-term health. Plus, if you want your child to be physically fit, the best thing you can do is to be physically fit yourself. Model what you want to see your child doing.

Spiritual Well-being

Our spirituality can also be dashed when faced with our child's substance use. Spirituality is related to our deep, sometimes religious, feelings and beliefs, including a sense of peace, purpose, connection to others, and thoughts about the meaning of life. It can also include an internal experience—a mindfulness or meditation practice, for example. Many of us have come to know spirituality as connecting to something bigger than ourselves, or finding inner peace in nature. We all have our own definitions of what spirituality means to us: traditional religion, eastern philosophies, mindfully experiencing nature, daily readings, or meditation. For those connected to an organized religious group, prayer can bring comfort. You can talk to others who share your beliefs, and volunteer your time. All of these connections can help you ease the pain of what you are going through.

Spirituality is also associated with improved mental health, managing substance use, marital functioning, parenting, and coping. I've often heard it said that the key to long-term change is support from others and a spiritual practice.

When we find something that addresses the spiritual aspect of our lives, it can relieve much of the stress that we are feeling. Our spiritual connection often starts with trust, respect, kindness, and affection for ourselves.

If traditional spiritual practice is not for you, there are many other ways to improve your mental health and reduce your stress and anxiety levels. Meditation, for example, is a tool that can help you think more clearly and increase your happiness levels. It's free, easy to do, and has plenty of positive side effects, including helping with medical problems such as cancer, chronic pain, asthma, heart disease, and high blood pressure. You need only a few minutes each day to get started.

As friend and fellow coach, Leslie Ferris Yerger says, "The more you take care of yourself — the better off your child will be!"

Two Quick and Easy Mindfulness Strategies

Along with meditation, consider trying one of these two mindfulness exercises to help bring you back into the present moment. Dr. Russ Harris, author of *The Happiness Trap: How to Stop Struggling and Start Living: A Guide to ACT,* offers the Ten Deep Breaths technique.

Take Ten Breaths

1. Throughout the day, pause for a moment and take ten slow, deep breaths. Focus on breathing out as slowly as possible, until the lungs are completely empty, and breathing in using your diaphragm.
2. Notice the sensations of your lungs emptying and your ribcage falling as you breathe out. Notice the rising and falling of your abdomen.
3. Notice what thoughts are passing through your mind. Notice what feelings are passing through your body.
4. Observe those thoughts and feelings without judging them as good or bad, and without trying to change them, avoid them, or hold onto them. Simply observe them.
5. Notice what it's like to observe those thoughts and feelings with an attitude of acceptance.

It's not uncommon to get caught up in your thoughts when trying to focus on your breathing. When I tried this exercise, I instead acknowledged my thoughts and let them go by. Dr. Harris says that many of us "get hooked" by our thoughts which is what often happens in life as well. Our thoughts pull us away from what we are doing. This exercise trains you to get yourself unhooked from your thoughts and focus again on your breathing.

You will learn from this exercise (1) to let your thoughts come and go without focusing on them and letting them distract you, (2) to notice when you've been "hooked" by your thoughts, and (3) how to "unhook yourself" and refocus your attention.

This exercise can be particularly helpful when you are worried about your child and find yourself getting lost in your thoughts and the what-ifs.

Set Aside Time to Worry

Another idea that may be helpful is to set aside time each day for worry and negative thoughts. Give yourself a specific time where this is all you focus on.

First, visualize yourself putting all of your concerns into a box with a lid that closes, then placing it in a closet where you won't see it too often. Then, at a predetermined time, or if your negative thoughts are running off with your day, mentally pull your "worry box" off the shelf. Spend some time mulling over all the worries—no more than a half hour. Then, visualize closing the lid on the box and putting the container back on the shelf until the next time. When your allotted time for fear is over, try to focus on thinking positive thoughts, being optimistic, and feeling hopeful.

You can also redirect your attention by wearing a rubber band around one of your wrists. When you feel yourself focusing on the negative thoughts, gently snap the rubber band and refocus on more positive thoughts. It doesn't help your emotional state to continue to play the broken record of what-ifs.

Writing

With all the time we spend with technology these days, it's easy to get disconnected from our inner selves. When we focus on our goals, values, and beliefs, we feel better. It helped me to keep a daily journal and read inspiring books.

In *The Artist's Way,* Julia Cameron talks about what she calls "morning pages." "Put simply, the morning pages are three pages of longhand writing strictly stream-of-consciousness."

Julia says, "Anyone who faithfully writes morning pages will be led to a connection with a source of wisdom within. When I'm stuck with a painful situation or problem that I don't think I know how to handle, I will go to the pages and ask for guidance."

I find the three-page limit helpful: a clear starting and stopping place. Three pages is doable.

Writing about what's on your mind takes it out of the realm of negative mind chatter and onto the paper. It's a place to express the anger, frustration, and fear, and a way to learn patience and understanding.

In his book *Writing to Heal*, Dr. Pennebaker says, "People who engage in expressive writing report feeling happier and less negative than before writing. Similarly, reports of depressive symptoms, rumination, and general anxiety tend to drop in the weeks and months after writing about emotional upheavals."

If you feel traumatized by your experience with your child's drug or alcohol use, see if you can take a few minutes and write about it. Sometimes that's all that's needed to help move you through your grief and on to the rest of your day.

Writing has been very helpful to me, especially during the tough years. It can be a source of new ideas, a place to express your feelings without judgment. It can be a way to connect to your inner being, a doorway to your innermost thoughts.

Dr. Pennebaker, in his book, *Opening Up by Writing It Down: How Expressive Writing Improves Health and Eases Emotional Pain,* explains, "Find a quiet time and place for this next writing exercise. Write for 20 to 30 minutes, focusing on your deepest emotions and thoughts about a stressful or upsetting experience in your life. Whatever you choose to write about, it is critical that you really let go and explore your deepest emotions and thoughts. Write continuously, and don't worry about spelling, grammar, or style.

"*Warning:* Many people report that after writing, they sometimes feel somewhat sad, although this typically goes away in a couple of hours. If you find that you are getting extremely upset about a writing topic, simply stop writing or change topics."

Dr. Pennebaker goes on to say, "Ideally, pick a time at the end of the workday or in the evening when you know things will be calm and quiet. Promise yourself that you will write for a minimum of 15 minutes a day for at least three or four consecutive days, or a fixed day and time for several weeks (for example, every Thursday evening for this month). Once you begin writing, write continuously. Don't worry about spelling or grammar. If you run out of things to write about, just repeat what you have already written."

If your child is in a treatment program, most likely they will be writing about their experiences and feelings. There is a reason for that—it gives your child a way to express their feelings. Give it a try; you may find it helps you as well, and it's a way to connect with them when they're away. Even if you write only a couple days a week, you may find yourself feeling better once you can get all of the heavy stuff out of you. This is a small investment to feel happier and less stressed.

Modeling Self-Care

There are many aspects to self-care, and many ways to avoid feeling overwhelmed and depleted. Again, when you practice self-care, you model the same for your child—you give them an example to follow as well as tools to help themselves.

It's also helpful for your child to know that you can take care of yourself, independent of what they are doing—it's one less burden for them. When you take care of yourself, you will be operating from a healthier place. You will be clearer about the decisions you need to make.

Once you start to care for yourself, your child may begin to do the same. We see this play out often: your decision to get off the emotional roller coaster starts the healing process.

Some ways to start the process are to reach out to others in the form of professionals and group support. There are traditional and evidence-based support groups in every major city. I found two parents' groups in my hometown when I was first starting out. It was comforting to connect with the parents who were also dealing with their child's substance use.

Some parents mix both the traditional and evidence-based approaches so they can get as much information as possible. There are other groups now in many cities across the country that parents and coaches have put together. For example, I have a monthly group for parents that comes with my online course. Attending a group meeting connects you with others who are dealing with the same problem so you don't feel isolated and alone. Also, I encourage parents to take a patchwork approach. Learn what you can from the different approaches and see what works for you, as every situation is different. As the 12-step slogan says, "Take what you like and leave the rest."

A word about support for your child: As you model reaching out for help, your child may feel encouraged to do the same. Alcoholics Anonymous and Narcotics Anonymous are well-known support groups, and it is helpful that meetings are available in every major city. So if your child resonates with the 12-step approach, they will easily be able to find a meeting. Yet the 12-step approach isn't the only way to find recovery. One mom mentioned that she kept pushing her son to attend an AA meeting, when he was telling her that they didn't work for him. Rather than assume that your child doesn't want to change, this could be a time to listen to your son or daughter and know there are other options. SMART Recovery, Women for Sobriety, and Recovery Dharma are some alternatives that offer an approach that your child may find more helpful. She Recovers is another wonderful support for women and continues to expand their reach. They now have group support specifically for Black, Indigenous, and Women of Color, LGBTQI+, women who are veterans and first responders, and more. Check the Resources at the back of the book for links to find these groups and others that you may find helpful.

A Father's Story

I listened to an episode of the Sober Conversations podcast a few years back, and it stuck with me. Dr. Herby Bell, a chiropractor, created Sober Conversations to spread awareness around addiction. While Dr. Bell has stopped producing new shows, there are many interesting and helpful episodes on this podcast. One in particular impressed me: an episode in which a father named Dennis discussed how he was dealing with his daughter's addiction.

Dennis shared that the most important thing he could do for his daughter, who was still in the midst of her addiction, and his family was to be healthy himself. In the interview, Dennis spoke about the work he had done to heal himself, including group work, journal writing, and exercise.

I assumed that Dennis's daughter was in early recovery, because he sounded so calm. I was surprised to find that this was not the case. At the time of the interview, Dennis's daughter was sitting in a jail cell, with legal issues connected to her drug use. It was amazing to learn that this father was enduring the pain of his daughter's situation, yet was so in control of his emotions and reactions. His inner peace was inspiring.

He explained at one point that he had been asked to take in his grandchildren. His head said *no,* because this was not what he had pictured for this time in his life. But his heart said *absolutely*! He loved his grandchildren and would do anything to protect their health and safety. What he worked on, and what many parents work on when their children are struggling, is figuring out what they can and cannot do, and not feeling guilty about their choices. This is not an easy feat for those of us who have struggling children and feel pulled between guilt and resentment.

Creating Opportunities for Your Child

In 2006, about three years into my daughter's recovery, we decided to run a half marathon together. Thirteen miles sounded hard but possible to me, so I downloaded a training routine and started running. I was determined to finish this race and not embarrass myself or my daughter.

She had never been a runner, but wanted to give the race a try. My daughter trained as well, so she would be in shape to complete the race with me and some of her friends.

Both of us started slowly on race day, but as time went on, the runners thinned out and we found our pace. We ran together while her friends decided to go on ahead and meet us at the end.

About a mile out from the finish line, my daughter wanted to run ahead at full speed. I realized she could have made better time if she had run the race with her friends. She had chosen to stay with her mom, which was so sweet!

When she took off, I heard a cheer from the sidelines. I looked over to see a group from her former sober living home, there to cheer her on. That put a big smile on her face!

We crossed the finish line, both relieved that we had completed the race and were not the last ones to finish! It was an accomplishment, and we were proud of ourselves. We had pushed ourselves further than we had ever thought possible.

One of the things I love about running is the lessons that we can carry over to our lives. Over time, our small steps add up to large ones; by taking small action steps, our goals become doable.

I didn't think I would finish the race, but I managed to, one step at a time. All change is like that: one small step at a time.

Self-care is a critical piece of the healing process. We *want* to take good care of ourselves, yet we also know it can be easier said than done. Making an effort to start down that road can help you to feel better about all aspects of your life.

Self-Compassion

No one would dream of judging someone with diabetes or cancer. Yet judgment happens regularly with substance use. This can have a massive impact on your social and emotional health.

Suppose you feel you or your child is being stigmatized because the people you encounter aren't comfortable thinking about drug dependence. You may begin to internalize those negative feelings. This can develop into shame and doubts about your good judgment.

Debbie Hampton, author of the article "The Benefits of Self-Compassion and How to Get More," says, "Not to be confused with self-pity, complacency or arrogance, self-compassion involves acknowledging your own suffering, faults, and mistakes and responding with kindness, caring, and understanding, without any judgment or evaluation. It's talking to and treating yourself as you would a friend. It's seeing your troubles and screw-ups as part of being human."

Many families feel that they did all the right things. They are partnered, employed, and able to provide for their children in every way. They were helpful supports for their children and tried to be the best parents they could. And yet their child still turned to substances.

Some families struggle with every variety of family issues, yet produce children who are well-adjusted. We all know examples of both.

There are things that parents can do to help prevent substance use. *But if you're at the point where your child is already using drugs or alcohol, it doesn't help to go back and beat yourself up for all the things you think you did wrong.*

It would be more helpful if you could develop self-compassion. See if you can treat yourself as your own best friend. This will be an important tool for your long-term mental health, and your success in fighting your child's battle—and your own.

When you realize that your child is using drugs or alcohol, it often causes stress and anxiety. Rather than judging yourself harshly, try to see yourself as your kindest friends or family members would. Do what you can to stop being self-critical. What would you say to your friend if they were in the same boat? What would you do to help them? How can you take those same efforts of encouragement and support and apply them to yourself?

Self-compassion allows you to feel the pain of your situation without letting it take over your life. Forgive yourself for your past mistakes—learn from them, of course, but treat yourself gently. Do your best to move forward with a sense of peace and well-being.

Your child needs compassion, and so do you. Give yourself radical permission to let go of all the guilt and shame. It allowed me to focus on more helpful, positive things.

Compassion for Yourself

According to Kristin Neff, PhD, author of *Self-Compassion: The Proven Power of Being Kind to Yourself*, self-compassion entails three core components: self-kindness, recognition of our common humanity, and mindfulness. If we combine these three essential elements—which all happen to be of benefit to parents trying to be more compassionate with themselves and their children—we can learn how to be genuinely self-compassionate. Here are my thoughts on how this can apply to dealing with your child's substance use.

Be Kind to Yourself

Treating ourselves with kindness is an integral part of self-care. Yet the idea of being kind to ourselves is often overlooked. We are often our own harshest critics, berating ourselves at every turn for our mistakes. Instead, we can learn to be gentle and understanding with ourselves, rather than critical and judgmental.

With all of the stigma and shame attached to substance use, it's no wonder that we beat ourselves up for all the things we did "wrong" that contributed to our child's drug or alcohol use. Having a child with drug or alcohol issues puts you in a place where you may feel judged by others. You may also harshly judge yourself. But the more loving and kind you are to yourself, the more confident you will feel, and the wiser your decisions will be during this anxious time.

Treat yourself as your own best friend. Pat yourself on the back for the hard work you are doing to help your child. Remind yourself that you are a kind, responsible parent. Be mindful of your inner critic. Do you criticize yourself for failing because of your child's issues? We often have had little or no training as parents, and knowing what to do if our child decides to experiment with drugs or alcohol is a complicated endeavor. It is essential to learn to give yourself a break from time to time.

Be as gentle with yourself as possible. Begin to notice what you did right when it comes to parenting to balance out any ongoing, negative inner dialogue. Some days you may have nailed your parenting. You were ready with the appropriate dialogue or action that helped your child at the right moment.

Other days you may have felt busy, overwhelmed, or tired. Maybe you didn't pay enough attention or weren't dialed in, or you snapped at your child. Know that you're not alone. We are all just doing the best we can with each situation that arises. Of course, it's important to strive to be the best parent possible. Every child deserves that.

You don't have to look far to realize that everyone is struggling with something. You may look at your neighbors and friends and think they have the ideal family, with perfect kids—but that ideal exterior might cover up problems that you aren't aware of, such as financial issues or health problems. It's easy, especially on rough days, to fall into self-pity. Many of us have felt that way at certain times. An alternative, which can be challenging, but something to consider, is to ask yourself, "What is my lesson here?"

I have found that when parents suffer with their child's painful experiences, it can be life-changing. And even though it hurts to feel the pain of your child's substance use, you can still help your child and be proactive.

Our Connection with Others on the Same Path

When we feel connected to others rather than isolated by our suffering, it changes everything. The truth is, we're not alone, no matter how much it might feel like it. And feeling connected to others and remembering that others are going through the same thing can be a strong foundation for healing. Connecting with others who understand the pain helps to lessen the stigma and shame, and leads to the realization that you really aren't the only one in this situation.

We cannot heal from the trauma of addiction in a vacuum. Though it may seem counterintuitive, I have found that the more self-compassionate I am, the more often close friends and family reach out to offer support. Perhaps this is because they see me being kind to myself and that makes them want to be kind to me too; maybe they see me taking care of myself and the situation and they feel less overwhelmed by the idea of reaching out to help.

Staying connected allows you to feel less judged. You will be able to share everyday experiences with others who have empathy and compassion and learn from other people. Compassion means "to suffer with." By connecting with others, you will have the opportunity to hear their stories, and come to feel and understand their pain.

You will also have the chance to receive compassion from others who have walked before you. Studies have shown that those who receive support of some kind feel less anxious and depressed. Feeling connected is positive for your physical and emotional health.

Having a child whose behavior feels out of control can leave parents feeling helpless and frustrated as they look for answers. You may feel outside your comfort zone. It's tempting to focus on the past.

Instead, see if you can start a new habit of focusing on the positive behaviors that your child *is* engaging in. Consider what positive changes you can make to improve your life. Find other people who can support you and your family.

Self-Love

We can lose sight of loving ourselves because we often blame ourselves unfairly for the problem. We do need to do the work to be self-aware and open to how we can address issues in the best way possible. Yet self-love starts with having compassion for yourself. Living through the pain of your child's substance use feels chaotic and complicated, and life often feels out of control.

How can you encourage compassion for yourself when you have many emotional up-and-down moments? You may have many conflicting feelings that you are trying to deal with such as guilt, shame, frustration, confusion, anger, fear, and disappointment.

Bringing in love and kindness for oneself can be a challenge. Yet, you deserve to have understanding and compassion just like anyone else.

The more you replenish yourself, the more able you will be to handle whatever comes your way in the future. Keeping calm and keeping balance in your life will help you lessen your stress. You will feel more in control of your life and be more at peace with your family situation. And you will be a role model for your child and other family members.

Focus on the Now

If your child is doing well, or if things are at least stable for the moment, see if you can appreciate that. If you feel that your child is struggling, remember that this is a temporary situation. Every situation, every mind-state or feeling, will shift if you give it time. As Rumi says, "No feeling is final."

Do what you can to help yourself in *this* moment, and to be patient with yourself and your kid. Encourage yourself by giving yourself positive feedback. Remind yourself that you are a good person. You have helped your child before, and you can help them now.

Later in the book, we'll get into ideas about how to reward your child, but the foundation is laid when you learn to reward yourself *first*. Accept that you are having a hard time, and try to be your own best friend by, say, bringing some joy into your life.

If you are struggling to shift your mentality, try writing down some of the negative things that you say to yourself. Then ask yourself, "Is this how you would talk to a friend?" Remember, even small shifts in mindset and behavior can help you feel much better.

While it is hard to let go of the dream you had for your child, holding onto it will only cause you to suffer more. Let go of the past. Help yourself and your child live for today.

Case Study: Gail and Sean

Gail had a good sense of humor, although she was in pain because of her son Sean's drinking. "I'm so stressed, " she said. "I've been going through this for years with Sean. He goes along for a while and seems better, and then he starts drinking again. My life is a roller coaster, and it's exhausting."

Gail mentioned that Sean, 25, had been to rehab two years ago. He lived in a sober living home but then got kicked out because he started drinking.

Gail said she had no support because she was too embarrassed about the situation. She lived in a small town in Georgia and didn't want to go to an Al-Anon meeting since she might have run into someone she knew. She owned a business in the city, and everyone seemed to know everyone's business; she didn't want people talking about her. She was beginning to have health issues of her own, which she thought could be because of her stress.

Gail committed to walking at least around the block every day. As the days went by, she walked for at least 30 minutes several times a day. Gail realized how refreshing it was to get outside. During the walks, she had time to think about things that would help her, and could take a break from worrying about Sean. She got some breathing room.

She felt relieved that she had reached out for support and was considering attending a meeting. The pandemic made it easier because they were online, and it was less likely she would run into someone she knew. She also decided to try out a SMART Recovery Family and Friends meeting.

Gail and Sean's dad offered Sean several options for getting help. Sean decided to try a therapist in town who specialized in substance use, who had a men's' group that he ran each week in his office, and Sean tried a few different kinds of meetings to see if any of them resonated with him.

Gail felt a shift happening. Sean was on a better path, and they both felt more comfortable discussing the issue in a calm, more compassionate way. Gail didn't know what the future would bring, but she felt more hopeful than she had in a long time.

Chapter Summary

- You will be a role model for your child and be more resilient when you are proactive about self-care.
- Take yourself on a conscious journey of self-discovery, personal growth, and self-development.
- Addressing your emotional, social, physical, and spiritual health will help you stay grounded.
- Activities such as regular exercise, meditation, deep breathing, and writing your feelings down can help.
- There are many options available for support.
- Develop self-compassion. Treat yourself as your own best friend.

PART 3: CONNECTING

CHAPTER 5

Changing the Conversation

I've learned that people will forget what you said, people will forget what you did, but people will never forget how you made them feel. —Maya Angelou

Since finding CRAFT recovery, our communication is improving. I am so grateful for that! —Andrea K.

One of the foundations of the CRAFT approach is learning better ways to have more effective conversations with your child. When we discover that our child is using substances, fear and anger may rise to the surface. The atmosphere at home can become filled with tension. You may feel that you are walking on eggshells to avoid conflict and find it difficult to say anything positive. Starting to focus on the positive things their child is doing rather than just the negative has been a turning point for many parents when they apply tools they learn through CRAFT.

But confrontation, yelling, and anger lead to more suffering for all involved. When confronted, kids often become defensive and belligerent. Stress and anger can lead to you blurting out words that you'll regret—and hurtful words are not easily forgotten.

These exchanges may affect other family members as well. Siblings may hide in their bedrooms, trying to stay out of the fray. Spouses may retreat as well, if the stress of the situation is too much.

The other downside to conflict is that you, the parent, become the problem. Your child can tell himself that your nagging is the issue, rather than their behavior.

Positive Conversations

Positive conversations are the key that unlocks the door to change. If you can take the time to talk with your child about the issues, to listen to him or her without lecturing, you'll both begin to hear each other in a new way.

Having a productive conversation with your child is the launching pad to connecting with them in a more positive way. Your young adult or teen will be more open to listening to you when your conversations are more pleasant.

Positive communication connects you both, and that connection is vital. You will create the opportunity to be on the same team as your child, to solve the problem together rather than fight against each other. As one mom put it, "My son started to change when I changed the conversation."

Listening to Your Child

Listening to your child is one of the ways that things can really start to get better. It is so tempting as a parent to take the role of advice-giver, because you have life experience. The answers seem obvious. At times, I've had to bite my tongue so I wouldn't jump in with my advice. What I have found is that sometimes just nodding is effective.

Even though your child is struggling, they still have something to say. They have reasons for their struggle and a voice that wants to be heard. See if you can give the gift of listening without judgment.

In his book, *The Journey of the Heroic Parent: Your Child's Struggle and the Road Home,* Dr. Brad Reedy states:

"Pack your lectures and your solutions and your analogies away unless your children specifically ask for them, and instead just learn to be present with them. This is what it means to nurture. This is what it means to love and to be a good parent.

"I have felt no greater joy, intimacy, or connection than when I have been on the listening side of such an exchange—both as a parent and as a therapist. I believe that if we can learn to be with our children in this way, then when they struggle and want help, they will be more likely to approach us for help than to hide their pain away."

Listening is a critical piece of the positive conversation puzzle. After all, what is the point of having a conversation if we are not listening to each other?

But How?!

You probably already know that having great conversations with a young adult or teenager can be challenging, even under normal circumstances. In the chaos of a home devastated by drug or alcohol use, listening, staying calm, and talking through issues may feel impossible. You might wonder: How do I listen, stay calm, remain nonjudgmental, and work together as a team when my child is stealing money out of my wallet or taking Grandma's jewelry to buy drugs?

Still, I encourage you to try to at least keep your mind open about where the conversation will go. Try to go in with no agenda except to hear what your child has to say.

Positive exchanges can begin the process of staying close with your child. These types of conversations can lead your child to be more willing to seek help—and that process takes time.

And timing is critical for having a conversation. When your son or daughter is drunk or high, it's not the time to have a substantive, productive chat about their substance use. Having these conversations when you are both in a calm emotional state allows you to hear each other.

When you notice that your child is willing to listen and engage with you, you can attempt to keep the conversation going. Keep it positive, as best you can.

If your child is not interested in talking with you—if they yell, swear, shut down, or criticize you—this is a sign that it's time to stop the conversation and save it for another time. The less you engage in negativity with them, the better. While it's understandable that you are anxious to see change, plowing through when your child is upset is unproductive and can harm the relationship.

Angry outbursts or your child shutting down can push the problem further into darkness. The damage and breach of emotional trust that occur during an argument can be hard to recover from. They may retreat. These adverse outcomes may get in the way of them being willing to talk to you the next time.

Practice Makes Progress: Tips for Success

When you need to talk with your child, think through what you want to say ahead of time, and do your best to keep it brief.

See if you can practice using more positive conversation strategies. Sometimes having more consistent, if brief, positive conversations can bring forth the results that you want.

No matter what you do, your child will be the one to make the ultimate decision about how they want to live their life. But with a few tweaks to how a conversation is approached, possibilities may begin to emerge. Everyone involved will feel less stressed and more open to listening. Change can "magically" occur.

Open-Ended Questions

As with any topic of conversation, when you are talking with your son or daughter about their substance use problem, it helps to ask open-ended questions that cannot be answered with just yes or no. An easy way to think of it is to try starting your question with words such as *What* or *How*. It's an opportunity to start a discussion, rather than allow a one-word answer to stop things in their tracks. Your kid may feel less defensive or backed into a corner when you ask these types of questions.

Some examples are: *What would be the benefit of change? What do you need now that will help you stay on track? How can I be of help?*

Ask if the Time is Right

Another strategy that helps is to ask your child ahead of time if they want to talk. When your child has the chance to decide if the time is right to talk to you, you're less likely to run into the roadblocks of anger and defensiveness. This also helps kids to feel more engaged, like they're part of the conversation and not just being talked "at."

This can feel awkward at first. One mom wondered why she needed to ask permission to talk to her adult daughter when she was living in her home, and she was paying all of her expenses. But I've noticed that when I ask first, it's a more helpful way to share a comment, make a suggestion, or even ask a question, because I see increased attention and more interest in the conversation. My child's antennae go up. They are listening and curious about what I have to say.

Waiting for the right time also gives you the opportunity to think through what you want to say. When talking to my kids, even today, I often reframe what I'm going to say so it's more upbeat. I want to be sure I'm coming from a place where they will not feel judged.

You can practice this, like many of these skills, by asking to have a conversation with someone you are not particularly concerned about, like your spouse or other children. You may find it works wonders with them as well!

Keep It Short and Sweet

Another suggestion is to keep your information or question short and to the point, and then follow it up with something like, "Does that make sense?" Or "Do you want me to explain that in a different way?"

I have seen firsthand that the long-winded approach doesn't work. My kids often tuned out before we were halfway through a conversation. I've also sent very long emails to both my son and daughter about how concerned I was about their situations. I'm sure they never read most of those emails.

I've come to realize that if you say it once, it's a suggestion; if you say it many times, it becomes nagging. And nagging doesn't feel good for anyone.

Changing the subject can be one of the most helpful things you do.

Reflective Listening

Reflective listening is a tool that can be helpful whether your child is in the midst of their substance use or in recovery. It can help with any conversation.

Reflective listening is about letting your child know that you heard them. It's part of listening without judgment.

The next time you have a conversation with your child, try to just listen to what they say and the feelings that they convey. Reflecting on what you hear, repeat the exact or approximate words you heard, and/or the emotions you heard. Like this:

"What I heard is that you feel _______________ (an emotion, such as sad, excited, nervous, relief, annoyed).

Or

"What I heard you say is________________________."

You can then check back to see if you were correct: "Do I have that right?"

You don't jump in and try and fix the problem. You don't offer suggestions unless you are asked. You're just present, and you listen. Also, ask questions for more information, if you want to learn more or if you are unclear.

Finally, you may want to offer to help: "Is there anything I can help you with?" "Do you need any help?" The beauty of this is that you are allowing your child to take responsibility and make the decision about whether they need your help or not. It makes them feel more empowered and in charge of their lives. One of the greatest gifts you can give your child is to listen to them without judgment or trying to exert control.

Validate and Empathize

It helps to validate and have empathy for your child's experience. A young person struggling with substance use can often feel invalidated by their parents and other family members. When talking with your child, let them know that you accept them for who they are, even though they are having a hard time.

Try to convey an understanding of your child's point of view. Maybe you had the same feelings when you were your daughter's age. When you let her know you understand how she feels, and that those feelings make sense to you, you both will feel better and your child will feel heard.

Showing empathy will set you up to change together, as a team. You and your child will feel like you are on the same side. Expressing your understanding doesn't mean you agree with her actions—what you are saying is that you understand her feelings.

The relief your child feels could be huge. If you're willing to try to understand your child's experiences without judging her, your child may begin to feel less defensive—because she realizes that you understand how she feels, and you care. This connection builds empathy and helps the relationship, and the better your relationship, the more likely it is that your child will listen to you and be willing to change her behavior.

Some examples of what you could say are, "I know you feel stressed because you are trying to find a job. That must feel like a lot of pressure on you right now." Or "I know you are having trouble getting an appointment. That can be frustrating." Do your best to listen without judging.

Crystal Clarity

We may not be used to giving a lot of thought about the way we talk to our kids. But when you are concerned about your child, it helps to put some thought into the conversation. That way, you won't miss an opportunity to get to the heart of the matter.

I know it's hard to bite your tongue. So often, as parents, it is crystal clear to us that a change here or there could make a world of difference in how our child functions in the world, yet while we can help, they need to come to this realization themselves.

When I have been able to get clear about the behavior that I wanted to change and explain what I want in such a way that my child understood what I *wanted* him to do—rather than what I *didn't* want him to do—it worked better. Being clear gets better results.

For example, when my kids lived at home, I worked on stating what chores I wanted them to do, so everyone was clear: "Take out the garbage once a week and empty the dishwasher when it's clean." When my kids moved out of the house, I thought about other ways to be more specific, such as "I would love it if you'd call or check in at least once a week." I have found that the more specific I am, the less confusion there is all around.

Focusing on the behaviors you want, rather than those you don't, also helps change the conversation from being critical to being supportive. It lessens the chance of your child being defensive as well. Keep an eye out for something positive your child is doing well or that you appreciate about him or her.

Dr. Robert J. Meyers explained in my interview with him that "One of the biggest pieces of CRAFT that helps the most is that we teach them how to re-communicate in a very positive way. We talk about giving them understanding statements or statements of empathy, like saying, 'I know it's been hard on you, and I know this is difficult, but I really would appreciate it if you could spend a little more time with your kids, or a little more time with working on your homework, or whatever it might be.'

"Instead of going in and saying, 'You never get your homework done,' you go in and say, 'I know this is difficult for you. Would you like me to help you? Would you like me to help you get a tutor? What can I do to support you in getting good grades and working on your homework?'"

Showing Your Feelings

A question that comes up often with parents is, "Should I say how I feel?" If your child agrees to meet you somewhere and they are a no-show, do you remain quiet or express your frustration? The fear for some parents is that they may not see their adult child again for a long time if they express their feelings.

I think it's important to express your feelings. You can and should let your child know how you feel. But try to stay calm and unemotional. If you are feeling highly emotional, see if you can take it down a notch, to keep the negative emotions to a minimum. For example, rather than saying you were feeling terrified, dial it down to something like, "I was worried about you." The key here is not to let things escalate into an argument. Just simply state how you feel in as calm a voice as possible.

Take Some Responsibility for the Problem

If guilt gets in your way—as it got in mine, for many years—know that you are not to blame for your child's substance use. Yet, shouldering a small part of the responsibility will let your child know that you and your child are in this together.

Our children are the victims of their childhood situation, as it is out of their control for the most part. Maybe you feel now that you overcommitted to work and were not present when your child needed you. Or maybe you were dealing with a substance use issue of your own at one point in your child's upbringing. It helps to let your child know that you are willing to own up to your part in the problem. When you begin to work on yourself and realize that the issue involves the entire family, you will all do better.

Playing the Victim

We often hear stories about the negative behavior of people addicted to drugs or alcohol. They may steal, lie, disappear for days at a time, miss appointments, miss important life events, and on and on.

Let's say it's a given that you're on the receiving end of some of these challenging behaviors. You will suffer *the most* because of them if you feel like your role is that of a victim, just reacting to what's being done to you. If you're so focused on how all of this is affecting *you,* you get stuck in victim mode—and you can't make any positive changes from that place.

See if you can change your story so that you are not seeing yourself as the injured party. Instead, become the proactive parent who is stepping up to deal with this unfortunate turn of events. Even through your pain, you can take steps to make things better—and implicitly, this means you're *not* a victim.

Accept That You Don't Always Know What's Best

So often, when parents are faced with their child's need or problem, they jump in and make suggestions for solving the problem. Instead, try just asking your child, "How can I help?"

This gives your child the responsibility of deciding what he needs. Asking how you can help instead of taking charge shows your child that he can solve problems and empowers him for the next time. If he isn't sure how you can help, then you can use your best judgment around healthy ways to support him.

Present a United Front

As much as possible, present a united front to your child. It removes the excuse that Dad and Mom disagree, so the child doesn't have to follow through. Kids of any age do better when they are getting the same message from both parents. I'll talk about this more later.

In my years of coaching parents, I've found that parents are less depressed and more hopeful and empowered when using positive conversations to help their child move forward. And in my personal parenting journey, I have found that using these techniques really helps to keep my relationship with my kids close. I feel closer to them than I think I would have been if I had not learned how to talk to them in a more inclusive and thoughtful way.

After talking with your child, you can ask yourself: Did I learn anything new about my child? How do I think my child felt about the conversation?

Case Study: Cheryl and Jessica

Cheryl's daughter, Jessica, was 29 years old and addicted to alcohol. She had been in and out of two rehab programs and finally went to sober living, then drank after having been sober for almost five months. She got herself back on track with a new therapist, a job, and an apartment. Jessica then had to move back in with her parents, because she lost her job and then her apartment during the pandemic. This change was very hard on her.

Jessica wanted to believe she was not an alcoholic and she could control her drinking. She had had two incidents of drinking and driving, and experienced seizures from alcohol withdrawal. She had spent time living on the streets and been in jail. Her parents thought she was doing better, but after she had been home with them for about a month, they came home to find her passed out on the living room rug.

They had a vacation planned but had to cancel it since they weren't comfortable leaving her alone in the house—they were worried they'd come home to find that she had been drinking, and that she could have a seizure while they were away.

Because of her age, they had little influence to get her to go to rehab voluntarily. They were defeated, tired, and emotionally drained.

Cheryl felt that her conversations with Jessica were overly emotional, and that her nagging could turn into yelling. Jessica would shut down, and there seemed to be constant tension in the house. She was worried for her daughter and missed how close they used to be.

Cheryl decided that instead of coming up with solutions for Jessica's problems, she would let her know she was there for her if she needed help. She realized that she should put as much energy into herself as she put into Jessica's problems. If she could plan some self-care time each day, that would make her feel better.

Even though Cheryl was tired of dealing with the situation, she decided to try noticing positive things Jessica was doing. Her interest in going to school and getting a job were both steps in the right direction.

Cheryl made an effort to try to change the way she approached Jessica. She tried to be as positive as possible and enjoy some fun times with Jessica. As time went on, Jessica started to reach out to her mom more often. They took walks together and went to lunch occasionally.

Jessica agreed to continue seeing her therapist, who she liked and connected with. There were more extended periods when she wasn't drinking, and the doctor helped her stay safe through the process. Jessica also joined a local women's recovery group and started to connect with a couple of the women.

While Cheryl knew they weren't out of the woods yet, she felt Jessica was making progress. She was feeling better about her relationship with Jessica, and she felt more confident in her ability to talk about the problem without Jessica feeling judged or shamed. Cheryl continued to learn new ways to connect with Jessica, be empathetic, and have more compassion for her daughter's struggles. At the same time, Cheryl found ways to help herself and enjoy time with her husband.

Chapter Summary

- Confrontation, yelling, and anger lead to more suffering for all involved.
- Changing the conversation to one that is more positive will makes it more likely your child will be open to getting help for his or her problem.
- Listening to your child is a critical piece of the positive conversation puzzle.
- Staying connected to your child is vital.
- Accept partial responsibility for the problem and do your best to present a united front with your spouse or partner.

CHAPTER 6

The Larger Family Unit

Live so that when your children think of fairness, caring, and integrity, they think of you. —H. Jackson Brown Jr.

In an ironic and twisted way, my son's addiction, as painful as it has been for me, is also the gift that completely changed my life. —David C.

The ripple effects of addiction reach and impact all family members. Your other children and your spouse will also need help from you to navigate their emotions. Substance use is painful and exhausting for everyone, but the more you help each other get through this critical time in your life, the better. CRAFT reminds us that collaboration helps with stress and sends a clear, positive message to your child.

Parenting Styles

Our parenting styles, which may influence how we approach the problem, are in turn influenced by how we were parented. We decide whether our parents' approaches benefitted us or not and go from there.

Parenting is an imperfect science. Many of us feel that we are amazing parents one day and not so great the next. Most people do the very best that they can. While it is life's most complex and important job, there is no such thing as perfect parenting. Like anything else, you learn from your mistakes.

Some of us are more strict, and some of us are more lenient. But it turns out that neither being too strict nor being too lenient is the best parenting strategy. Somewhere in the middle is usually the most effective approach. Since these are not normal or ideal circumstances, your style may change to suit the situation.

The better you understand what your parenting style is, the more self-aware you will be. Here are some parenting styles to consider.

Controlling. The controlling parent ranks low in responsiveness to the child's needs and wants. They usually demand that the child follow marching orders issued by Mom and/or Dad. The rigid parent places a high value on conformity and compliance. Little input from the child is sought or allowed. The parent imposes punishment, and the child seldom faces the natural consequences of her choices. The decree is: "Do it because I say so."

Permissive. The permissive parent is high on responsiveness to the child's every whim and ranks low in requiring accountability from the youngster. Permissive parents often rescue their children from experiencing natural consequences. The child may even have the final say in family decisions. Household rules are often fuzzy and erratically enforced. The feeling is: "I wish you wouldn't, but do what you want."

Uninvolved. Uninvolved parents are low in responsiveness and low in demands. This parent appears indifferent, distracted, cold, or even rejecting. The uninvolved parent is often emotionally and/or physically unavailable to the child. There are few rules and few logical consequences. The uninvolved parent often defers decision-making or, when making a decision, pays little attention to the child's response. Uninvolved parents rely on teachers, nannies, or the juvenile justice system to manage their child's growth and well-being. The clear message is: "Do what you want. I don't care."

Authoritative. Firm but fair, authoritative parents set realistic limits and insist that the child adheres to them. They provide appropriate warmth, affection, and mutual respect, but children know that the ultimate authority resides with the parent. The child receives both logical and natural consequences. The understanding is: "I love you unconditionally, but there are boundaries in our relationship."

We all fall into different parenting styles at different times, yet we usually have a general approach that we operate from most often. As you may have guessed, authoritative is overall the most effective parenting style. Being loving, fair, firm, and consistent, even during troubled times, will give you the best chance of moving your child forward in a healthy way.

I grew up with parents who were loving, but more on the controlling side, especially my mother. She had pulled herself out of a low-income family situation as a child, become a nurse, and enlisted in the army during World War II. I'm not sure if her experience influenced her parenting style, but she felt that discipline was the main way to raise a child. My dad was more easygoing, but for the most part went along with her approach.

My upbringing influenced me in that I tended to be more lenient with my kids. I was more easygoing than my mother and didn't want my children to feel the resentment that I had felt at times as a kid, growing up with strict rules. Yet at the same time, how I was raised was always in the back of my mind. It helped me remember not to let things go and to have boundaries.

Do you know what your parenting style is? What has worked well for you in the past, and what would you like to change going forward?

Parent-to-Parent Communication

Communication between you and your child's other parent may feel strained if you each have your own ideas on the best approach. Again, this often comes from the way you were raised as a child. Taking the time to work through any of your childhood difficulties may support you both in coping better with your child's substance use. Talking with each other and finding common ground helps.

Working as a team will help you present a united front to your child. As you work through the issues surrounding your child's use, each parent will bring his or her background to the problem. The more you can work together toward helping your child change, the better.

I've sometimes seen a dynamic in which one parent has more of a tough-love approach, wanting to enforce harsh consequences. The other parent wants to use a more compassionate approach and is uncomfortable with harsh tactics or sometimes without any rules at all.

What can help is to talk about how you can meet in the middle. Even if you don't agree on everything, consider one or two areas where you can find agreement. Start by using those ideas to help your child make needed changes.

It's okay to agree to disagree, while supporting each other through the process. Getting some help with this is ideal, as it is difficult enough to parent a child who is struggling, and trying to work with a spouse or partner who disagrees with you can just add to the stress.

Throughout the process, the boundaries and consequences for your child must be clear and specific. It doesn't help if your child gets mixed messages, so try to work together as much as possible.

A few years ago, I talked to a dad, Greg, who was trying to create clear boundaries for his son, Ben, who was continuing to use substances. He and his wife, Carol, had discovered that Ben was driving under the influence with their car, and he wanted to establish a clear boundary around not driving the car. He didn't want Ben to hurt himself or someone else by driving high.

They held the boundary for about a week. One day when Greg was away from home at a meeting, Ben asked his mom if he could drive the car to work. Carol, who had a more challenging time with boundaries, gave in and let Ben use the car.

It was not the first time this kind of thing had happened, so as you can imagine, Greg was angry. He felt that Carol was undermining him too often and that Ben was constantly pushing against the boundaries he and Carol set because his parents couldn't agree and too often gave in.

Separation and Divorce

While couples often find that they are not in agreement with how to approach the problem, this difficulty can be compounded for parents who are separated or divorced.

Any kind of separation can be traumatic for your child. Their age, resilience level, and the circumstances will influence how your child reacts to it, but no matter how old your child is, separation is usually painful. What can make a parent happier doesn't necessarily make a child happier, and that can be hard to accept. While the partnership ends for the parents and they can often go on with their lives, a child feels the pain of the situation but has no control over what is happening—they may feel like the foundation is being pulled out from under them. If the parent enters a new partnership with someone who has kids, the child will then have new step siblings—another adjustment.

Judith Wallerstein, psychologist and author of *The Unexpected Legacy of Divorce: The 25-Year Landmark Study* states, "One in four children in this study started using drugs and alcohol before their fourteenth birthdays. By the time they were seventeen years old, over half of the teenagers were drinking or taking drugs. This number compares with almost 40 percent of all teenagers nationwide. Of those who used drugs, four in five admitted that their schoolwork suffered badly as a result. A majority used these substances for more than five years and several were seriously addicted by the time they reached their twenties."

It's critical that parents put aside their differences and do their best to work together to help their child when they're suffering. Some parents can work together despite their differences; sometimes stepparents prove to be helpful as well. Other times, not so much—and then one parent may be left to cope with their child's substance use alone. This only adds to the stress.

The following are two success stories about coparenting through struggle.

Marilyn's Collaboration Solution: All In

Marilyn's adult son had been struggling with different substances for a couple of years. Marilyn had divorced her son's dad and remarried.

When her son's substance use became apparent, Marilyn, her new husband, and her son's father decided to meet regularly to discuss the problem and work together to find solutions to it. They went to counseling appointments together and consistently stayed in contact—through the ups and downs of the son's substance use, relapses, and finally, his recovery.

They don't always agree on everything, but they talk things through and get help from their counselor when they need to, so they are presenting a united front to their son.

Katie's Collaboration Solution: Only Biological Parents

Another parent, Katie, whose daughter, Robin, was having an issue with drug use, had been divorced for several years and had remarried.

Katie's husband decided to take a back seat. He felt it would be better to let Robin's dad and Katie work with Robin to find solutions to the problem. He knew Robin's dad was very present in her life and would be the best person to help. For their family, that was the best decision.

They got some suggestions on where to start with Robin's treatment program. Despite several disagreements around the cost of the treatment programs they were looking at, they were able to work through their differences and support Robin during the crisis. It was critical that both parents stepped up and worked together. For the most part, they presented a united front throughout the process.

Both parents realized and were clear that Robin needed to get help as soon as possible. Parents coming together to help their child, whether they are married or divorced, can be key to a child's success in kicking the habit.

When you find ways to work with your partner or co-parent toward a common goal, your stress level will be reduced. You may feel more optimistic about your child's situation and be able to spend your energy on helping your child change rather than engaging in more conflict.

Yet the sad reality is that, for some families, this is just not possible. So whatever situation you find yourself in, just do the best you can.

Ten Basic Messages for Families

These positive messages are adapted from Dr. Meyers's CRAFT approach. They are helpful reminders as you stay focused on supporting your family.

1) **Research has shown** that family members can learn techniques to engage their substance-abusing loved ones into treatment or to living a healthier life.

2) **You are not alone.** You may feel isolated at the moment. Unfortunately, many other families also suffer from substance use. The success of these families solving their substance use issues can give you hope.

3) **"You can catch more flies with honey than vinegar."** It is understandable that you feel negative emotions because of drug or alcohol use. Yet, it is easier to get your loved one to listen to you when you talk in a positive manner. Remember what you do love about them. Focus on the positive changes you are interested in seeing.

4) **You have as many tries as you want** to work with your loved one to help them make better choices. Positive communication improves your relationship. People can be helped at any time.

5) **You can live a happier life** whether your loved one engages in a more positive lifestyle or not.

6) **When you help yourself, you help your family.** You become a positive role model for the rest of your family. Develop your resilience and work on having an upbeat, healthy attitude toward life.

7) **Neither you nor your loved one are crazy.** All people have problems, and substance misuse is just that—a problem. You did not cause it. Your loved one did not intend to become dependent on drugs or alcohol.

8) **The world is not black or white.** Every situation is different. Your loved one may be more interested in changing their behavior if presented with more than one option.

9) **Labels do more harm than good.** They are not helpful. Using the words *addict* or *alcoholic* can be a major barrier to seeking help for substance use.

10) **You have nothing to lose** and a lot to gain from getting involved.

Siblings

Substance use often affects siblings too. At the least, they likely feel the loss of attention and the disruption in the family. Some are embarrassed by their brother's or sister's behavior. They may have to face criticism at school or get excluded from social events because the family is now seen in a negative light.

The relationships between siblings may change, as brothers or sisters try to understand the substance user's erratic behavior. What may once have been a close relationship could deteriorate to a point where they may not recognize who their sib has become. Some find themselves feeling pressured to keep quiet about their brother's or sister's use. They think they will be betraying their sibling if they tell their parents the truth about what is really going on.

Also, they may disagree with how their parents are handling the situation—sibs have to deal with the pain of the problem but have the least amount of control over what is happening in their family. They may share their disagreement with you in unpleasant ways. They may feel resentful of the money that their parents have spent on treatment and getting help. On the other side, parents may worry that younger brothers and sisters will follow in their sibling's footsteps. Siblings often do influence each other when it comes to substance use, which complicates the issue.

Your other children may also be frustrated and confused by their sibling's behavior. Their pain can spill over into heated arguments with you, or they may take steps to avoid the situation as much as possible. Younger kids may not understand what's going on and may act out.

Sibs face many challenging scenarios when confronted with the substance use of their sibling. There can be much anger, shame, frustration, and resentment. Some feel the painful loss of their beloved sister or brother. They sense the despair of the situation but do not have any control, as parents are usually making the decisions. So they may struggle with how to help.

Or they may feel the need to tell Mom or Dad about what their sibling is doing because it seems dangerous—then they are left feeling like they've lost their sibling's trust. None of these scenarios is an easy place to be.

Dealing with substance use can be a turbulent time. Sibs are often caught in the crossfire. They may feel helpless and confused about how to best support the one struggling. They may be afraid that addiction runs in the family, and that they will suffer from it as well.

If the addiction has taken away the attention they usually receive, siblings may get fed up with the situation. They don't like seeing their parents in so much pain and resent the problems their sibling has caused. They may also feel shame or guilt if they decide it's better to let go of their brother or sister and not interact with them. The pressure to perform or be perfect so that their parent has less to worry about can be exhausting as well.

Being compassionate with your other children and partner (if you have one) can keep the family together and moving forward in a positive way.

Your other children may be feeling a confusing mix of love and resentment for their sibling. The relationship between your children can be strained at best. They may not want their sibling in their life anymore because of the pain, and yet they may miss the relationship and feel abandoned by their brother or sister. Some may have lost their role model and feel confused. Others may have lost a younger sibling to dependence on drugs or alcohol and feel guilty that they didn't do more. They often feel powerless and caught in the middle.

They may have peers at school asking about their brother or sister and not know what to say. They may find that they, like their parents, are not invited to parties—friends' parents may not want to have their children at their house because they're afraid the sibling will use drugs or alcohol too. Kids may find themselves now dealing with their sibling's reputation.

It's often hard for sibs to find someone they can talk to. They don't want to burden their already overburdened parents, so their emotional needs often fall through the cracks. Too often, everyone is focused on helping the parents and the child struggling with substance use, forgetting the sibling, who may be taking on new roles that they feel unprepared for, such as caretaker or protector.

Ten Hard Things for Siblings

Dawn Clancy, a journalist, grew up with a sibling who struggled with substance use. Here is her list of ten hard things about being a sibling of a person with an addiction issue.

1) **Your brother or sister chooses their drug of choice over you.** You call and they won't answer. You make plans and they don't show. They would prefer to drink or get high rather than spend time with you as a sibling, and that hurts.

2) **You don't trust that your sibling is sober when he says he is.** Many times, siblings will be told that their brother or sister has changed and that they are no longer using, only to find out the truth and be disappointed—again.

3) **You have a parent who enables your sibling, and it drives you crazy.** You may not agree with your parent's decisions, and you are put in the uncomfortable position of watching your parents make decisions that don't seem to work. It can be hard to watch.

4) **You love and hate your sibling.** You've watched the deception, lying, stealing, and other negative behavior that has hurt family members, to the point where your resentment, anger, and even hate are on the verge of bubbling over at any minute. While this is a normal way to feel, what you hate is the behavior. Your true sibling

is still there behind the drug use and when they change, the bad behavior will recede.

5) **You've had to cut your sibling out of your life and you feel horrible about it.** Siblings are put in a terrible position with addiction, where they have no control. At some point, they may feel that there is nothing more that they can do and cut ties with their sibling. Even though this may feel like the right thing to do, it is difficult. They may question themselves about the decision.

6) **You're always preparing for that phone call.** The dreaded phone call that parents fear can worry siblings as well. You feel anxious thinking about how your brother is dead, or your sister overdosed and was found lifeless under some bridge. That is stressful for anyone and something siblings live with every day when their brothers or sisters are in the midst of their use.

7) **You miss your sibling.** You may feel that you need to separate yourself from your sibling. It is painful. You miss who your brother or sister was and who they might still become. You miss those special moments with them that are no longer. Again, you have been put in a position where you have little or no control.

8) **You deliberately downplay your success.** You may feel guilty over the success that you've had in your life. When your sibling is struggling each day, you don't want to brag about what is going well in your life, and yet you want to celebrate and be happy about how well your life is going.

9) **You feel judged, like people think because your sibling is using substances, you are too.** Your sibling's reputation can haunt you, even as early as elementary school. Other parents may forbid their kids from socializing with you because they are afraid of the negative influence they feel you could have. While we know that addiction is

not contagious, many families are fearful and don't want their children associating with a family that has drug or alcohol issues. It can take years to heal a battered self-esteem and step out from underneath your sibling's shadow.

10) **No one understands what you are going through.** Many siblings grow into adulthood feeling isolated and alone with their shame. As siblings of people struggling with addiction, it is important to speak up and share our experiences with one another. Find groups and communities where others can relate to what you're going through.

Appreciating Your Other Kids

Your other children are likely suffering from their anger, frustration, and pain around their sibling's substance use, even if it's not apparent. Despite the fact that substance use can feel all-consuming, your other children deserve your time and attention as well. They may be doing many things right—you don't want to miss out on appreciating them because you are so focused on your child who is struggling.

Notice and acknowledge what your children are doing well. Spend quality time with them each day, so that they know that they are loved and valued. Even though their sibling has some serious struggles, they can be reassured that you are there for them as well.

Keep any discussion about their troubled sibling light and keep them informed in an age-appropriate way. Use the situation as a teaching tool for them to understand the dangers of substance use, so they will hopefully make better choices for themselves.

Stay positive and optimistic for your other children. Let them know that there is hope for their brother or sister. Make sure they know that they are not alone. Remind them that many other families struggle with substance use, so that they don't feel isolated.

They may have concerns about what to tell friends and other family members. Brainstorm with your spouse, partner, or older siblings how you want to approach sharing the information with others. There are no right or wrong answers.

Unfortunately, substance use can sometimes continue for years. You do not want your other children to remember their childhood only as a time when everyone was worried and frantic about their brother or sister.

Having compassion for all your children will allow you to be available to them when they need you the most.

Get Help

Support can be helpful for all family members. It can help sibs to understand what substance use is and how all family members are affected, and groups like Alateen can be helpful support. They may also benefit from professional help to process the situation, perhaps from a therapist or counselor, either alone or with the family.

As a parent, model good self-care and help all your children to understand addiction. Demonstrate that they, too, can use tools to help themselves cope. I would encourage your other children to get involved with the recovery process. The entire family is affected by drug use. Family therapy can be one place to start. It can be a place that gives your children space to express their feelings about the situation.

I would also encourage your other adult children to educate themselves about addiction. They may be frustrated that you are not using the tough love or other approaches that they've heard about.

Once they've educated themselves on the best ways to cope with substance use, there will be less conflict. It can be helpful for all involved to teach your other children to set boundaries for themselves and not cover up for their sibling. While this is not always easy, it can only encourage continued substance use. Some families feel the need to shelter children, especially younger ones, from the raw truth of what their older brother or sister is going through. That is a choice that you need to make as a family. When they are older, the more truthful you can be, the better. Younger siblings need to know about their genetic risk as well at some point as they enter the teen years.

Introducing them to the CRAFT communication strategies could be helpful. You can also practice the strategies on your other children, which is likely to be less emotional. Also, note that the CRAFT tools are helpful for any behavioral change you are seeking.

Case Study: Janet and Bob

Janet and Bob were parents to four children. By the time their youngest son, Marc, was 18, he'd had a drug and alcohol problem for a few years. They had tried several different approaches to help Marc, but he continued using no matter what they tried.

Their oldest son got into several arguments with Bob about the parents' decisions. One day, Janet came into the kitchen to find her older son, Michael, screaming at Bob to kick Marc out and let him learn his lesson. Michael felt Marc had ruined their perfect upbringing. Bob felt like he had PTSD with all the constant drama. He not only had the stress of Marc's substance use, but he also had to deal with the resentment of his three other children.

Finally, after catching him several times using drugs in their home, Janet and Bob gave Marc options of several treatment centers to attend. Marc decided to live with some friends for a while to think about what he wanted to do.

Janet and Bob reached out to him several more times, and they finally convinced him to go to a treatment program. He attended treatment but relapsed soon after leaving the program. Janet and Bob convinced Marc that he needed more help, and he agreed to go to another, longer treatment program.

Both of the programs were costly, as treatment programs usually are. Their other three children became more and more resentful about how much money their parents were spending on Marc, and how worried Marc had made his parents.

Once Marc had been in treatment for several months, Janet and Bob wanted their kids to mend fences so that they could be a family again. They struggled with how to help all their kids become friends once again and let go of their resentments around Marc's treatment.

When Marc finished his treatment program, he moved into a sober living home. He started to attend a few family dinners. Janet wanted Marc to call his siblings, but he never did. Maybe the shame was too much. As time went on, Marc continued to do well, and his siblings began to let go of their resentments. His sister, Janie, whom Marc had been close to, reached out to him, and they started to spend time together. Michael attempted to understand their parents' decisions and to welcome Marc back into the fold.

As time went on and Marc continued on his recovery path, his siblings became more open to him and spent time with him. He felt he needed to earn their trust back, which takes time. What Janet and

Bob wanted most was for their family to be whole, and slowly they were getting there.

Last summer, Michael got married. Marc was very much part of the celebration. He looked terrific—happy and engaged. Marc is now 21. He's been through a lot and has a long way to go, but thankfully he's headed in a better direction.

Chapter Summary

- There is no perfect parenting, yet it does help to understand your parenting style.
- Working as a team will help you feel less stressed and present a united front to your child.
- Things can be more difficult if you are separated or divorced, so the more you can work together, the better.
- Substance use affects siblings, who have to deal with the pain of the problem but have the least amount of control over what is happening in their family.
- Stay positive and optimistic for your other children and family members.

CHAPTER 7

Change

While it is not always an overnight change, it does occur. That message needs to be front and center. —Ken Carpenter, PhD

Even if our child should relapse, I've found it best to focus on the fact that this may just be necessary for him to experience so that long-term recovery is attainable. I always continue to love and support him in appropriate ways. Never give up! —Pat N.

The "Perfect Plan"

Think about the last time you tried to change your behavior. First there is usually some planning as to how to accomplish the desired change. Next there is some action—but the timetable is different for everyone. Some people take longer to decide to change.

Some in recovery say their parents were the reason they decided to change their life. Others found that they'd had enough of the negative consequences and wanted their life to be different. Either way, families can be a motivator to change.

Everyone is different, but one thing's for sure: being a positive force will make it more likely that your child will consider living a healthier lifestyle. And the sooner you intervene, the better, because there will be fewer negative experiences for all.

Yet change doesn't happen in one step; it occurs over time.

For a parent, this can be frustrating to watch. You get hopeful when your child makes progress, only to see those hopes dashed when they back slide. Your emotions feel controlled by your child's behavior. Their progress may continue, but it's usually not on your timetable. The process of change will test your patience, but the good news is that your child has recognized the problem and is moving in a more positive direction.

Consider where you think your child is right now.

- What is the change that you would like him or her to make?
- What would he or she need to do differently to make the changes you would like to see?
- How can you best support your child now?

Stages of Change

The Stages of Change Model was originally developed in the late 1970s and early 1980s by James Prochaska and Carlo DiClemente at the University of Rhode Island. They were studying how smokers were able to successfully give up their habit or addiction.

This model has since been applied to a broad range of behaviors, including weight loss, injury prevention, overcoming alcohol and drug problems, and more.

Here are the five stages and what you and your child could be going through at each stage. Keep in mind that these stages are not always linear, and that people approach change in their own way. The stages of change are useful because it can help you have more clarity about where your child is in the change process.

Precontemplation

For parents, this stage might look like the "out of sight, out of mind" approach to dealing with your child's substance use. You have an idea that something is wrong, however you are in denial that you need to take action. Don't be hard on yourself if you were here at one point. Most parents need time to accept what is happening to your child.

This stage is where your child is being demoralized. He may not know what to do and find it's easier to deny there is a problem. He has no plan to change any time soon.

You can help your son or daughter by having positive conversations, helping your child see the difference between where they could be and where they are now. Pay attention to his feelings, get facts about ways to change, and ask how you can help.

Contemplation

For parents, this is the stage where you may have experienced a few negative consequences of your child's substance use. You hope the problem will go away but realize that you probably need to take action. Yet you may still be on the fence because of fear, overwhelm, stigma, and shame.

In this stage, your child may be getting ready. He is thinking about the possibility of making changes. The pros of change are coming to light and your child begins to realize that change might be helpful for him. Ambivalence is quite common, and your child may be held back by fear of failure.

This is a time when you can look at ways to lower the barriers to change which I'll talk about later in this chapter.

Preparation

For parents, this stage is when you realize that action needs to be taken. You may choose to look into treatment options, look for professional help, check your insurance benefits, find a group meeting and look into medications that might help. You may also read a book or two on addiction, check out websites, or call family or friends who have experienced substance use with their young adults or teens.

Your child is ready to take action. They may begin taking steps to get there by going to a meeting, consider talking to a counselor or going to treatment, and overall getting clear in their mind that they are ready to change their life.

Your encouragement and love helps. You can support your child by helping her create a plan of action, look into treatment options and stay positive.

Action

As a parent, this is the time when you are ready to act. You know your child has a problem. You're in a stage of acceptance of what you are facing and are ready to step up and help.

In this stage, your child "takes the plunge," and is ready to move in a direction of moderation or abstinence. Your child may decide to see a therapist, go to detox, enter a treatment program, attend a group meeting, change their phone number, engage with sober friends or find other ways to change their life.

You can help build confidence, use positive reinforcement, and review your environment for anything that might be triggering to your son or daughter. You are ready to lean in and support your child in a healthy way. You are engaging with resources to find out what could be the best fit for the situation.

Maintenance

For parents, your life will feel calmer. You are able to engage with your child and not be constantly worried about him. You are staying positive, noticing what your child is doing well and continuing to use the conversation skills that help your child feel good about himself.

Your son or daughter has been living a healthy lifestyle for about six months. They may be sober or able to successfully moderate their substance use. You can support your child by helping them plan ahead and build their confidence. You continue to reinforce their accomplishments.

Relapse

Relapse into old habits can happen for parents as well. For a parent, you may fall back into nagging or let your anger get the better of you. You also may have allowed your worrying to get out of control. It is understandable when it does. You can get back on track at any time and help your child get back on track. You can get back to supporting your child's recovery, not their addiction.

Relapse can happen and I know it's hard to take. Typical relapse rates for substance use disorders are 40% to 60%, which is characteristic of other chronic medical illnesses. Encourage your child to look at relapse as a learning opportunity rather than as a failure.

No matter what stage your child is in now, they can change their life. Long-term change is possible for anyone. As I've mentioned before, there are millions who have made positive changes around their substance use, and your child can be one of them.

Barriers to Change

Dr. Jonah Berger, the author of, *The Catalyst: How to Change Anyone's Mind,* states that "Rather than taking a predetermined plan and pushing it on people, catalysts do the opposite. they start by asking questions." This idea holds true with struggling teens and young adults. As the CRAFT approach suggests, the more we push, nag, and repeat the same information over and over, the more frustrated we become. And your child will be less likely to embrace the change you want to see.

In my case, we had numerous discussions about the negative impact of drugs and how they could affect all aspects of my kid's life. Hopefully they heard some of it, but often the words went in one ear and out the other. The earlier you intervene, the better, yet think about how you can approach the topic so that your child hears you.

Lecturing—which is a response that many parents jump to without giving much thought to better options —may result in an argument or a blame game. Your child may respond with something like, "If you'd stop nagging me, I wouldn't have to get high."

Stepping Stones to Change

First, when we push our children to stop using drugs or alcohol by nagging, threats, or repeating the same information over and over, they tend to push back. This is similar to the idea of taking a particular side in a discussion with your child. He or she may feel inclined to take the opposite side whether they feel that strongly about their position or not. So, consider ways of having a discussion with your

and give your child time to think about it. Again, these are baby steps that will move your child closer to the change that you want to see.

Your child is attached to how drugs and alcohol are solving their problem. Even though most of our kids realize they need to change, for a variety of reasons they are not able to. It's easier to keep using substances than to face the uncertainty of change. The positive benefits of change have to be clearly better than what they will have to give up for them to be willing to consider taking that step. Change takes time and effort.

Even though their life may be chaotic, they have a familiar lifestyle, friends and a way to solve their problem for the moment. To go through the challenge of changing their life, of not only having to go through the cravings, but also giving up friends and a lifestyle that they are used to is hard. When they don't know if they will be successful in recovery, it can feel overwhelming.

Fear of failure can get in the way, so reminding our kids of their strengths helps. Think about when they were younger and all the things that they could do well. Even though they may not show it, our kids don't want to continue disappointing their family and others who they care about. They may feel unsure about how to pick up the pieces of their broken lives.

Like anyone, your child wants to know that they will not fail and not be uncomfortable during the recovery process. Your child wants to know that change will be a positive experience for them and worth the effort. Right now, your child has a sure thing. Their drugs or alcohol use is a way to solve their problem. It is always a risk when we think about changing a habit. If it is too much of a risk, your child will most likely not consider letting go of their substance use. It's always easier for anyone to stick with what they are doing now, until it becomes too problematic.

What you can do is to help your child see the benefits of change as opposed to what they've got going on now. This is why allowing your child to feel the consequences of their substance use is key.

If what you are asking your child to do is too big of a leap from where they are right now, your chances are lower that they will be interested. They may not consider it because the change is too great. This is where harm reduction can be helpful. Ask for less of a change rather than pushing for abstinence. Abstinence is sometimes the only answer, but harm reduction can be a stepping stone. Invite your child to take a small step so that what you are asking for is something they would consider doing. Sobriety may not be something your child is willing to consider today. Yet starting with using less and lowering the risks of overdose is a good place to begin. Taking smaller steps toward change will help your child move forward and not feel overwhelmed. Remember that baby steps lead to big changes. This can look like trying moderation with alcohol first and getting support around that. Or agreeing to wean off the harder drugs and smoke marijuana instead. Everyone is different so getting professional help with this is important, yet harm reduction can save lives.

According to Dr. Berger, "It's really about *chunking the change.* Breaking big tasks into smaller, more manageable chunks."

So, what can you do? How can you help your child be more willing to consider change? Meeting with a counselor or going to a support group might give your child a taste of what support could look like. It's not as big of a change and they can start to get some help. Once they've talked to a counselor who they trust and feel comfortable with the process, they may be more willing to give an Intensive Outpatient Program or inpatient program a try if it is needed.

The more comfortable your child feels about how change will make a difference in his life, the better. He needs to feel that it will be worth the effort. While your child has heard you talking about the dangers of the continued drug use many times, it can be helpful to hear the same message from different people who your child trusts and respects. Hearing it from someone else who has been down the same path and who your child can relate to, can lend a different perspective and one that may be more appealing.

Also, labeling your child an addict or an alcoholic can hinder the change process. These are negative labels, and your child might be less inclined to get help if they must be labeled. This may be another barrier to change that isn't necessary.

What you can do now, is to lean in and continue the conversation in a positive way. Keep communication lines open with your child. Talk to him, listen to him. Try out different resources to find what seems like the best fit for your situation. Have patience, as I know the worry now becomes "Will he relapse?" Yet, you can influence your child, no matter what their age. There are many ways you can support your child's change in a healthy way.

For parents, your life will start to settle back down now while you continue to take care of yourself and stay resilient. Continue to practice positive conversation strategies at this time. It will help you to stay close to your child as they move forward in their life. Continue to reinforce the positive behavior that you see and allow for natural consequences safely.

Long-term change *is* possible for anyone. Millions have made a positive change around their substance use. Your child can be one of them.

Create a Supportive Structure

According to James Clear, author of *Atomic Habits,* "Changes that seem small and unimportant at first will compound into remarkable results if you're willing to stick with them for years. We all deal with setbacks, but in the long run, the quality of our lives often depends on the quality of our habits. With the same habits, you'll end up with the same results. But with better habits, anything is possible."

When substance use hit our family, I realized that change had to begin with me. I needed to begin the process of change for our family. I know I would have done things differently, especially if I had known where we were headed. I wanted to give my kids a stronger sense of self and solid tools so that they could navigate through the challenges of life. But what if it was too late?

Everyone is different. Our kids need different approaches to help them cope. If you can understand what your child may be thinking or feeling about his substance use problem, you'll be in a better position to help—knowing the *why* can make all the difference.

What would your son's life work be if he knew he couldn't fail? What would your daughter do if she found a career that she loved? Find the answer to that question, and then see if you can put things in place to help them move closer to their goals. It's hard to let go of old habits if you don't have anything interesting to look forward to.

When you have tried to make changes, what obstacles did you encounter? Did you have a sense of ambivalence at times? Did you question whether it was worth it? Your child is probably going through the same thing.

Case Study: Maggie and Daniel

Maggie was concerned about her son Daniel. She joked through her pain that Daniel had been on "an extended camping experience." The reality was that Daniel was homeless because of his ongoing drug use. He attended a dual diagnosis treatment in Palm Springs, but unfortunately relapsed on the plane ride home.

Daniel had used various drugs and was not willing to address his continuing drug problem no matter what Maggie and her husband tried. They decided that their son could not live at home any longer. He was not obeying their house rules and was unwilling to get help.

They felt exasperated, and because Maggie had been told that the right move was to let go and detach, they asked Daniel to move out, hoping that he would decide to get help.

But instead of getting help, Daniel ended up being homeless. No matter what negative things he experienced, getting help for his substance use did not seem to be on his radar. As time went on, Maggie grew more concerned about Daniel's safety.

Maggie considered visiting her son. She wanted to keep the lines of communication open but had been told that it was enabling.

When Maggie's husband, Don, had an upcoming business conference near Daniel, they decided to try and reach out to him. When they saw him, they realized that waiting for him to hit rock bottom wasn't working. Daniel wasn't getting better. He looked unhealthy, and he seemed to be going downhill. It was getting close to the holiday season and Maggie felt they needed to intervene.

Daniel was twenty-three at the time, and he still felt like a kid despite being of legal age. The terms of the Thanksgiving plane ticket, "Come home now, no questions asked, offer expires in 24 hours" marked a turning point in their relationship. He was by then quick to smell an entrapment scenario brewing. But Maggie had let go of that agenda. Not only did it not work the first time, Maggie also didn't have the money to try a treatment program a second, third, or tenth time.

Daniel did come home and agreed to stop his heavy drug use. Maggie didn't like Daniel's occasional drinking and smoking marijuana, but she stood by her decision to allow Daniel to come home. Maggie continued to have compassionate, positive conversations with him about her concerns. She also continually reminded him of all the positive things he was doing.

Eventually, Daniel took a part-time job. Daniel started to pitch in and help around the house, which she reinforced. They worked together to continue to explore options for Daniel. Their days were filled with a few steps forward and a few steps back.

Yet, Maggie felt frustrated at times because he had no clear direction for his life. She considered what boundaries would be appropriate and how she could be supportive.

As time went on, Daniel's behavior began to improve, along with their relationship. She felt that reaching out to him, being patient, and having compassion for him made a difference.

Maggie would have preferred that Daniel be sober, but she wanted to give him some time to figure things out. He wasn't always successful, but he continued to make efforts to eliminate hard drug use. He was functioning and was able to attend his college classes.

As he pursued a subject in college that he had been interested in, he felt like his life was coming together. His future began to look brighter, with clear direction and purpose.

There were several starts and stops for Daniel. He relapsed on several occasions. Finally, Maggie suggested that Daniel move out on his own to experience life as an adult. He had saved up enough money to pay the deposit for an apartment. Maggie and her husband agreed to pay the first month's rent to help him get started.

Daniel continues to work at staying off harder drugs. Maggie and Don are there to support him if and when he is ready to be sober. They are hopeful that as time passes and Daniel continues to feel better about himself, he will live a healthier life that doesn't include drug use.

Maggie's long game was to help Daniel stay alive in the hopes that he would survive long enough to mature a little. She felt extremely lucky; he celebrated his thirtieth birthday this month.

Today, he has been in the same job eight months, pays his own bills, has an apartment in his own name, and enjoys restored relations with the family. Most days, Maggie feels peaceful and engaged with her own life first.

They are, however, happy to have their son back, appreciative that their relationship is close, and that Daniel continues to show signs of improvement.

Chapter Summary

- Change doesn't happen in one step; it's a process that occurs over time.
- The Stages of Change Model will help you understand where your child is in the process.
- Your encouragement and love do make a difference. Notice the change that your child is trying to make and do your best to stay positive.
- Having a parent who is listening and gently nudging their child toward change is a gift.
- It is more helpful to lower the barriers to change than to push your child towards change.
- Harm reduction is another helpful option that can promote change.
- Long-term change *is* possible for anyone. Millions have made a positive change around their substance use. Your child can be one of them.

CHAPTER 8

The Power of Positive Reinforcement

Baby steps are key—baby steps and lots and lots of praise. —Erica Spiegelman

The positive reinforcement and staying connected to my child has been the BEST advice I've heard. —Amelia B.

Positive reinforcement is a powerful approach that can turn a negative environment into a positive one. It is one of the foundations of the CRAFT approach. Using positive reinforcement can powerfully change the tide—just by acknowledging the positive things that your child is doing. When your child is rewarded for their good decisions and behavior, they will make those same good choices more often. And positive reinforcement heals your relationship with your child too. Win-win!

Positive reinforcement can help shape and change your child's behavior no matter if they are a teen or an adult. When you see your child doing something positive, reward them in some way, such as with your words or a more tangible item that would be meaningful to them. Positive reinforcement motivates your child so that positive behavior is more likely to happen in the future.

If you ever used praise or treats when your child was toilet training or gave them money as for their report cards, you have already used positive reinforcement. And it can work at any age.

Jeff Foote, Carrie Wilkens, Nicole Kosanke, and Stephanie Higgs state in their book, *Beyond Addiction: How Science and Kindness Help People Change,* "You may have seen a *New York Times* article that went viral in 2006, 'What Shamu Taught Me about a Happy Marriage,' describing a woman's success using animal training techniques on her husband. Besides being funny and cute, it illustrated the power of behavioral strategies, particularly positive reinforcement, to promote change. People aren't dogs. Or rats. Or orcas. But reinforcement is a staple of some of the most effective therapeutic approaches with humans. People, as well as other animals, like treats."

As Robert J. Meyers and Brenda L. Wolfe state in their book *Get Your Loved One Sober: Alternatives to Nagging, Pleading, and Threatening,* "The old saying 'You catch more flies with honey than with vinegar' neatly sums up what rewards are all about. If you want someone to do something, give him a reward for doing it. Make that person feel good. The more often and powerfully someone is rewarded for behaving appropriately, the more likely she is to repeat the behavior."

Look for the Good

Encouraging baby steps can help instill the change you are looking for. Your support and encouragement are so needed. Your child needs to know that you are on his side and will be there to encourage him every step of the way.

For example, if your teenage son or daughter stays home for a night instead of being out with friends who will be engaging in substance use, let them know how much you appreciate their presence. If your daughter shows up for a family dinner and is sober, let her know you appreciate her efforts. If your son returns your phone call or text message, acknowledge his action in a positive way.

I have heard from parents on occasion that they feel their child is too old for positive reinforcement. But positive reinforcement works for a person of any age. Some parents think their teens or young adult should be doing these things already. Even if you do feel that these actions are things your child should already be doing, accept that this is where you are with your child. Reinforcement works and can influence change, so why not try it?

Your child may not be where you'd hoped in life. But regardless, when you notice what they are doing well, you demonstrate that you accept them for who they are, flaws and all.

Change can happen when everyone involved changes how they approach the problem. Annoyance, anger, and resentment can turn into compassion, understanding, and positivity. Change takes time. There will be steps forward and steps back. With patience, effort, and support, it will happen.

Please help your child by being a positive role model, acknowledging any acts of positive behavior, and staying optimistic, even when it's not easy. As Dr. Meyers says, "Change is a journey, not an event. It doesn't happen overnight. It happens over time."

What Motivates Your Child?

For positive reinforcement to work, you must offer a reward that your child values. Drug and alcohol use is itself reinforcing. Your child gets something back: their drug use, which is often pleasurable.

Is substance use helping him…

- feel less anxious or depressed?
- feel better about himself?
- fit in?
- something else?

To motivate change, you can counter the motivation and reinforcement from his drug of choice with another equally powerful positive motivator. It can take time and several attempts, but it is worth the effort.

Ask yourself what the reason for your child's substance use is. They are getting a reward, and it's solving a problem for them. If you take away their drugs or alcohol, their reward is also gone. What can you put in its place so that they are getting a reward for changing their behavior?

The idea with positive reinforcement is that you are offering something that can compete with the rewards of their substance use. Your child will feel good after receiving an acknowledgment from you, which could be comparable to how they feel when they are using substances.

Substance use helps numb the pain around trauma, anxiety, depression, other mental health issues, or other things they're struggling with. Your child generally doesn't feel good about themselves and is unable to pat themselves on the back, so it helps to have you, as their parent, come up with ways to acknowledge the behavior you want to see.

You are reminding them that they can do positive things with their life. They can make good choices. You will be improving the chances that your child will listen and be open to your advice.

That's Great, But…

Now, I get that positive reinforcement may sound good in theory, but most likely, you are feeling frustrated, angry, scared, and resentful about your child's continued experimentation or growing dependence.

You may be wondering…

Why aren't they beyond this?

Why do I need to reward a child when they should be doing these things already?

And w*hy do I need to reinforce my child who is struggling when my kids who are managing their lives don't need this kind of reinforcement?*

You may feel that your child should already know how to do tasks and behaviors appropriate for his or her age without your input. You also may be just exhausted by it all.

Manage Your Expectations

The reality is that your child is struggling now because of his or her drug or alcohol use. Expectations will not be the same as they may be for siblings or other people of the same age who manage their lives well.

People struggling with drugs or alcohol have nothing to give to you or anyone else, including themselves. Your other children, who are doing well, probably have inner strength and self-compassion, and can pat themselves on the back from time to time.

You may have been told that doing anything nice is enabling. But, for your struggling child, positive reinforcement can be a powerful way to encourage change. It will give your struggling child the chance to see that he can do something right, no matter how small.

Positive reinforcement is one of the most promising strategies. It makes so much sense. The best part is that it can really turn the tide on substance use—I've seen it time and time again. Many parents continue to use positive reinforcement with their child in recovery and extend that to siblings who may need support in other areas. Positive reinforcement is helpful in any relationship.

This strategy comes down to acknowledging your child when they are doing something positive and affirming that you want to see them do that again. It makes everyone feel better.

The More Specific, the Better

Decide what behavior you want to see in your child. Make it specific so that it is clear in your mind whether he is doing the behavior that you would like to see or not. Identify or make a list of things you feel your child would appreciate as a reward for their changed behavior. It could be a favorite dinner, some time alone, a gift card, or maybe tuition for a class they are interested in. Don't pick things that you would like your child to want or that you would want. Choose something that *they* will appreciate. Words are very effective too, so you don't have to spend money.

Positive reinforcement has the power to get your child back on track. It doesn't have to be expensive or take up a lot of time. Brainstorm some ideas that feel right for you. Keep the list handy so that you are reminded to notice what your child is doing that you appreciate.

When you notice behaviors that deserve a more significant reinforcement, such as staying sober for a week or landing a job, you can do something more. It is about noticing what they are doing right and shining some light on it.

You don't want to feel that you have become your child's handler. At the same time, evidence has proven that positive reinforcement is a powerful motivator to get your child to change. Rather than staying in the loop of your child's negative behavior, coupled with nagging, yelling, or withdrawing, using positive reinforcement can move you all forward to a better place.

Any change starts with baby steps. There will be small actions and small rewards. Don't lose sight of that fact. Don't lose patience or give up if you don't see immediate results or significant changes. Positive reinforcement is one strategy that can move your child forward to a better place.

Reinforcement, but not Bribery

You may be asking yourself, *But what is the difference between reinforcement and bribery?* I've heard parents make promises such as using the car, money, a place to live, etc., if a child stopped using, agreed to get help, or went into treatment. If offered ahead of time, it becomes a bribe rather than reinforcement. That's a slight distinction, but a big difference.

Bribery is a pattern that may have taught your child to act out to get what they want. And now it may seem like a decent option, to reduce risky negative behavior.

Bribes often occur when we're desperate for our child to change. But bribing them is a negotiation that gives your child the power and leaves you feeling powerless as you try to come up with bigger and bigger bribes the next time. This pattern results in resentment and anger. One parent reported to me that she had offered her son a bribe. She did her part, but her son did not follow through on what he had agreed to, which led to much frustration.

Reinforcement is different. The key here is that positive reinforcement is given *after* the action has taken place, not before. Do not suggest a reward ahead of time. Instead, when you see the action, immediately follow up with an appreciative comment or a reward.

Notice when your child does something positive that you've wanted to see. Acknowledge it with a hug, a smile, a thank you, a gift card, or whatever feels right to you. Reinforcers help your child feel appreciated and motivate them to continue with their changed behavior.

Change the Tone

When you give your child attention for what they are doing well—even when you have to look hard for these behaviors—it can begin to turn a negative situation into one with more positivity and hope.

Examples of behavior you can reinforce for your adult child who is living on their own:

- returning phone calls
- being sober for visits
- getting and/or keeping a job
- completing college classes
- working on lessening or stopping their drug or alcohol use
- staying with their recovery program

Examples of behavior you can reinforce for an adult or teen who is living at home:

- helping around the house
- finishing homework
- coming home for dinner on time

- helping with younger siblings
- walking the dog
- mowing the lawn or shoveling snow
- making meals for themselves and others
- getting a job and/or getting up each day to go to work
- working on lessening or stopping their drug or alcohol use
- staying with their recovery program

It is more challenging to verify what your child has done when they don't live at home. Use your best judgment, as you know your child best.

When you notice positive behaviors and appreciate them, your child will feel good. Though they are small, these are opportunities that you don't want to miss!

One mom was concerned about her teenage daughter who had taken up drinking alcohol. They sometimes liked to give each other a foot rub when they watched TV. She found herself sitting on the couch rubbing her daughter's feet when she knew she had been drinking. This is subtle, but she realized she was unconsciously rewarding her daughter for drinking. After we talked about it, she immediately stopped the practice when she suspected her daughter had been drinking. Instead, the foot rubs only happened when she knew her daughter was sober.

Counter Disappointment

Your child is wrestling with the stigma and shame of their drug use. They know they've not only disappointed you, they've also embarrassed you. No one wants to feel like they've let someone down, especially their parent.

Your child is most likely disappointed in themselves, even if they don't admit it. Pride and denial can get in the way of realizing that you've taken yourself down a dangerous road, especially when you are fearful of change.

If your child is never allowed to feel that they've done anything right, what is the point of trying to change? Being more positive reminds your child that they deserve your respect and have something to offer. Again, it is understandable if this feels challenging to you. Yet, it helps all involved to approach substance use in the most positive way possible.

Chapter Summary

- Positive reinforcement, which is one of the foundations of the CRAFT approach, is a powerful tool and can turn a negative environment into a positive one.
- The idea of positive reinforcement is that you are offering something that can compete with the rewards of your child's substance use.
- This strategy comes down to acknowledging your child when they are doing something positive and affirming that you want to see them do that again.
- Be specific about what you acknowledge. General cheerleading isn't so helpful.
- You will feel better yourself when you start looking for things that are going well.

CHAPTER 9

Consequences

With boundaries, it comes down to this, that you don't support the illness, you support recovery. —Christopher Kennedy Lawford

I have made crazy decisions out of fear but have gradually been implementing consistent boundaries over the past 12 months and my son (and I) are better for it. Boundaries were the hardest thing for me. —Lyn L.

One of the things that comes up often for parents is how to step back and let our children take responsibility for their actions. We must tell our son or daughter that we love them and will support their good choices. But it is also essential not to get in the way of the negative outcomes from their substance use. The Parent's 20 Minute Guide states, "When you shield your child from the uncomfortable result of his actions, he learns there's no downside."

It's better to step out of the way and let your child feel the consequences of their substance use. Allowing for consequences is the other foundation piece of the CRAFT approach. When you let your child take responsibility for their actions and reinforce the behavior that you want to see, you will increase your chances of seeing change happen. No matter how old they are, your child must experience the connection between their behavior and the consequences of that behavior.

Tough love can feel punitive both to the child on the receiving end and the parent implementing it. Often the messages are to let go and detach—in other words, we are told to turn our back on our child. Again, this kind of approach can leave your child in free fall, with no support system at a time he needs it the most.

A more compassionate approach is to stay as calm as possible and not jump in and try to fix things for your child. It is not about being angry, punishing your child, confronting, or threatening. It's letting your child feel the brunt of their problems. And it is *hard.*

You may feel that you must intervene for the safety of your child. But your comfort level and safety need to be considered as well. Parents often struggle with legal issues, having their child lose a job, fail a class, or jeopardize their chances of going to college. But, when you intervene on his behalf, you set the stage for your child to depend on you to bail him out of the negative situations in which he finds himself.

Pros and Cons

It can be helpful to weigh the pros and cons of the situation. If you don't cover for your child when they miss school or work, they may lose their job or jeopardize their future opportunities. But your child's experience with feeling the consequences of his behavior can have a profound impact. If the consequence is something you cannot live with, you should do what feels right for you and your family.

Just keep in mind that one of the cons of that decision is that your child may learn that you will take care of things, which won't motivate him to want to change his substance use. If you are there to fix every problem that arises, there will be no reason for your son or daughter to want to stop.

If stepping back from helping to cover up or solve the situation feels challenging, you are not alone. But it doesn't help our children in the long run if we protect them from a crisis of their own making. You may worry that your child's problems will forever ruin their life if they are left to run their course: grades, their ability to get into college, and their current or future job prospects can be affected. It can be frightening to watch your child's life fall out from under them.

Please support your child's change, not their continued substance use. Your child must experience a downside to their behavior. If you continually rescue them from their negative situations, there is no motivation for them to change.

And stepping out of the way does not mean that you are turning your back on your child. You can continue the conversation and be there to help.

Stay Calm and Start Small

To start, you can practice with something as simple as this: when they are late for dinner and don't call, dinner is not waiting for them. Your child can make or buy their own dinner.

Start small, with things you can live with, that will allow you to sleep at night. With any action, consider whether you are helping your child move forward or helping your child continue their substance use. It's a judgment call pretty much every time.

When you do step out of the way, be sure to do it in a nonjudgmental way. Try your best not to get angry, threaten, or confront your child. Sarcastic or negative put-downs are not helpful either. Ignore the behavior if it is safe to do so. Eliminate any positive reinforcement when you see negative behavior such as drinking or getting high. Your child will learn that there is a downside to using drugs or alcohol when they know they will have to step up and take responsibility for their life.

It's usually not helpful—in the long run—when you take it upon yourself to make sure your young adult is up on time to get to his or her job. Or if you cover for your teen by calling school, and making an excuse about why they're not there, or do your teen's homework for them, or make excuses for your young adult because you don't want to be embarrassed in front of your friends or family.

It is critical that your child be able to see that if she misses work, she may lose her job. If she misses school, her grades will suffer, and if she misses dinner, she'll need to make her own meal because no one is going to do any of these things for her. Stepping aside and letting your child suffer the consequences of their actions is best when done not in anger, but from a place of calm. You are simply stepping out of the way and letting the consequence happen.

And this does not mean you can't do anything nice for your child. As we discussed earlier, you can and should notice when your child is doing something well. You can still be nice. You don't have to be angry and upset with your child. In fact, the calmer you remain, the more you will be able to move your child forward to change. You will have the most power to encourage change when your emotions are under control.

Encourage behavior that you want to see, and step out of the way when your child has negative consequences because of their substance use, so that she can learn from it. Keep your child's safety and your stress level in mind as well. If allowing your child to feel the consequences of his use could jeopardize his personal safety, then you may need to step in. Or if your stress level will become intolerable, that's a consideration as well. Just be clear with yourself and do your best to stay out of the way. There are no guarantees, but with both of these strategies in place, you may be surprised at the changes that begin to happen.

Take a moment to think about your own situation. Are you supporting your child in a constructive way? Is there anything you are doing that might actually be supporting your child's substance use? You may find that you are solving too many of your child's problems.

Boundaries

Clear, consistent boundaries need to be in place to help your child because you will lose your interest in being compassionate when you feel that you have lost control. One boundary that most people agree is a good idea is to avoid giving their child money that they could spend on drugs or alcohol. If you want to support your child, you could cook or buy them a meal occasionally. Pay for other necessities if you want to, as long as you feel your support is not encouraging continued drug or alcohol use.

Some parents decide to forbid use of the car until their child is well on their way to recovery. The possibility of them driving high or drunk is just too dangerous, for themselves and anyone else they may encounter. If you decide to do this, you may feel that you are being punished because you have to drive your child to work, school or other activities. Something that can help is to agree to drive your child and have them do a chore for you in return.

Parents often ask about the cell phone—should I pay for it or not? Some kids who use continually lose their phone, so that can be a problem. Yet many parents do ultimately choose to pay for their child's cell phone, if only so they can stay in contact with their child. It's less stressful for them than spending sleepless nights worrying because they haven't heard from their son or daughter, or concerned that their child may feel isolated and alone with no way to contact them.

One mom realized she was doing too much. Her son would come home at all hours of the night, and she was worried he was hungry. She would get up at 1 a.m. to take him to a fast food restaurant that was open late, so that he could have dinner after spending the evening getting high with his friends. No wonder she was so tired! That is an extreme example, but it happens. She stopped and set a clear boundary when she realized what she was doing was not helping.

A boundary is the invisible line you draw around yourself. The line is drawn to protect you, the parent, and other family members—as well as the kid who's using.

If your child experiments or engages in risky behavior, you may, understandably, get angry and frustrated. You may get so caught up in reacting to the negative behavior that you lose control as a parent. As a loving parent, you want to feel compassion for your child and all they are going through.

But your feelings of empathy will quickly evaporate if you do not have consistent boundaries in place. You will feel resentful because the substance use has disrupted your life. It will be easy to feel overwhelmed when boundaries are not set up to help you protect your peace of mind.

It's hard to be consistent if you're not clear on your boundaries. Consider where you want to draw the line. What boundaries are important to you, your spouse, your partner, or your other children? Once we figure out what they are and communicate them clearly, we then have to commit to being clear and consistent about keeping them in place. It can feel like a lot of work, so I suggest choosing them wisely.

Boundaries are both limits and consequences for actions that you feel are inappropriate or unsafe. As we mentioned before, if your child doesn't experience a downside to their negative behavior, they have no reason to stop using substances.

To set appropriate boundaries for your kids, it's helped me to remember two things:

1. Set boundaries that you feel are appropriate for your child's situation. Every situation is different. Only you know what will help you and your child the most. Decide what your boundaries are and what the consequences will be for disregarding them. Collaborate with your spouse or partner, so your kids are getting the same message. Obviously, let your son or daughter know ahead of time what you want them to do so that everyone is clear.
2. Be consistent and follow through with boundaries and consequences. It doesn't help if you threaten your child with consequences and then fail to follow through. It is better not to set the boundary in the first place, because a lack of follow-through will damage your credibility. Your child will be confused about what they can and can't do. You may also find they are constantly pushing to see what other boundaries they can cross.

Do you remember parenting your child when they were a toddler, especially when it came to having to be consistent? Remember how they would just keep pushing if they didn't know where the limit was; if they cried or whined because they wanted something and you gave it to them, they learned that crying and whining got them what they want.

Your son or daughter is either an adult or close to being an adult. Yet emotionally they are younger. Their drug of choice keeps whispering in their ear that they need more. They need to keep pushing the boundaries to see if they are secure, because if they aren't, crossing them is a kind of shortcut to getting the high their brain is craving. You have been in this boat before and have a sense of what works and what doesn't with your child. Being consistent and supporting your child's recovery is the key to supporting change.

It can help to write down your expectations for your child and the consequence if they don't follow through. The more you plan ahead and think about the purpose of your boundaries, the better. Boundaries are not helpful when they are set in the heat of the moment, when it's hard to think straight.

Here are some things to consider:

- What do you want your day-to-day environment to look like?
- Who else are you concerned about in your home?
- What are your boundaries, and can you communicate them? Would it be easier to talk to your child or write them out, so you are both clear?

Boundaries are needed when your child is struggling and can't make good decisions. It's up to you to decide what you will support and where you draw the line. You know best what you can agree on and follow through on, so think through your situation and decide what will work for you.

Be Clear

As with the consequences discussion, here too it is wise to start small and save the heaviest consequence for later down the road. Some parents jump to thinking they need to kick their kid out of the house at their first offense. Here are my thoughts.

Asking your child to leave the home is definitely something you have in your toolbox, but it is something every parent should think long and hard about first. You can use that consequence one time. It should be the last thing you try when all else has failed, because many kids quickly go downhill when left on their own.

After being told to let her son go, one mom had to rescue her son from a homeless shelter in Florida and found him in very bad shape. As we all know, it's dangerous on the streets, and your child will likely end up staying with friends or acquaintances who are using drugs, sleep in a homeless shelter, or on the streets. That will not be a situation that supports any kind of positive change.

Also, once your child has left the home, it will be harder to communicate with them. They may have a phone, but they may be angry and not interested in talking with you. You will then no longer have an influence on them. All you will be able to do is just hope that they decide to change at some point.

So, I would tell your child to leave the house only when you've exhausted your other options and you've tried other strategies that keep them close and allow you to continue the conversation about getting help.

The other thing to keep in mind is that sometimes parents get into the habit of *threatening* that they will kick their kid out. When you don't follow through, it becomes meaningless and your child will no longer believe what you say. Again, you can tell your child to leave your home one time, so this is something to save until you are convinced there are no other options.

When you do, you need to change your locks and be sure there are no other ways for your child to enter the home. It is not helpful to have a situation where your child is kicked out and then he is allowed back and then kicked out again, and on and on. It becomes chaotic and does not help the situation, so think this decision through carefully.

And of course in instances where your child is being physically abusive, younger children are being harmed, or other intolerable situations, having your child leave may be what you need to do. Keep in mind that although your child needs to leave the home, he doesn't have to be homeless. Options such as a treatment program or a sober living home should be offered, so your child is getting help. Maybe a relative or a family friend who has experience in recovery would agree to help with the situation and provide temporary housing for your son or daughter with their boundaries in place. While this may be a rare option, it is something to consider as long as you feel the problem won't again get out of control. Sometimes someone with a little more distance who is knowledgeable on the topic can be helpful.

A written contract can help with setting boundaries, so everyone is clear. Your kids may be more likely to obey your rules when they are in writing. Others have written up contracts and found they didn't work because there was no follow-through. It can help to include your child so that you are all in agreement on the rules. Your child may come up with some things you haven't thought of. There is often more buy-in if your child is part of the process.

Boundaries are part of our lives. So rather than make the rules fuzzy, be clear.

While maintaining a close, positive relationship with your child is essential, your other role as a parent is to make clear, consistent, and fair rules, so your child will understand what is being asked of them and you and other family members are protected.

Parenting is complicated, especially when your child is struggling with substances. You can't solve all of your child's issues, but you can be clear about what you will support and where you draw the line.

Upholding Your Values

Your thoughts, ideas, feelings, emotions, core beliefs, values, and energy belong to you. In its simplest form, your boundaries hold together who you are as a person. It's like a fence protecting all of your resources.

So what happens when you have weak boundaries, or your child ignores your boundary? You will quickly start to feel that life is out of your control. When that happens, you will be drained and have no energy. Emotions can quickly feel overwhelming.

The key is to plan ahead.

Case Study: Anne and Jeffrey

Anne was a mom from Kansas, whose 21-year-old son, Jeffrey, had lived at home for the past year. He had been to a treatment program but continued to have issues with drinking.

Anne worried that Jeffrey was socially awkward. He was hiding out in the house, not socializing, and seemed detached from his friends. Jeffrey had had a job for a while and then was let go. He had started to attend college but had dropped out.

She was concerned too with Jeffrey's drinking and driving. For the most part, he seemed sober when he asked to use the car, but she had found empty bottles of vodka in the car on more than one occasion. She decided not to allow him to use the car, which only increased his isolation.

Jeffrey suffered from anxiety and depression. He was lonely, and Anne felt that he was in a lot of emotional pain. When Jeffrey was invited to a party or to go out with friends, Anne was torn. She thought it was good for Jeffrey to socialize with friends his age. But usually, there was drinking involved, and she continued to be worried about how much drinking Jeffrey would do.

She wanted to be supportive yet worried that she was being manipulated. She didn't want to kick Jeffrey out of the house, yet she didn't feel that he was making progress.

As time went on, Jeffrey continued to come home drunk too often for Anne's comfort. Anne finally reached a point where she'd had enough of the life that her son was content to live. She knew it wasn't healthy and was not helping him move forward.

She continued to acknowledge her son when he demonstrated positive behavior. However, if he came home drunk, she would not fix meals for him or help him out of any jams that he might have gotten himself into. She also made the decision not to eat dinner with him unless he was sober. She limited video game and TV use, both of which Jeffrey loved, and didn't allow him to sleep in every day. It felt strange to put these boundaries in place for a 21-year-old. However, Anne felt some additional pressure from her was necessary to make needed changes. She continued to be clear and consistent.

Anne just wanted her sweet, sensitive son to get his life back on track so that he could be the person she knew he could be.

Jeffrey began seeing a counselor regularly. He agreed to a meeting with Anne and the counselor after two days in a row of coming home drunk. During this session, they explained to Jeffrey all the positives of going to a treatment program. Jeffrey finally agreed to go to a wilderness program for young adult men. At first, he didn't like the program and tried to convince Anne to come and get him.

Anne stayed strong, and after another week, Jeffrey settled in, completed the program, and then moved on to sober living. The program suggested that Jeffrey be at least three hours away from home for his sober living program, and they both agreed that this would be in his best interest.

While Anne missed having Jeffrey close by, she realized that this separation was needed for him to internalize all that he had learned in treatment, and to experience a new way of being.

Chapter Summary

- Allowing consequences is the other foundation piece of the CRAFT approach. When you let your child take responsibility for their actions and reinforce the behavior that you want to see, you will broaden your chances of seeing change happen.
- Your child's experience with facing the consequences of his behavior can have a profound impact.
- Keep your child's personal safety and your stress level in mind as well. There are times when you may need to step in, but make sure that you are not giving your child too soft a landing.

- Clear, consistent boundaries need to be in place, both to help your child and to maintain your sense of control.
- A boundary is the invisible line you draw around yourself. The line is drawn to protect you, the parent, and other family members—as well as the kid who's using.
- Set boundaries that are appropriate and follow through.

PART 4:
GRATITUDE AND HOPE

CHAPTER 10

Treatment and Recovery

Nobody stays recovered unless the life they have created is more rewarding and satisfying than the one they left behind.
—Anne Fletcher

Recovery is life-long, and involves the whole family. There are challenging twists and turns: addiction is a physical, mental, and spiritual disease. We and our loved ones will be managing this chronic illness all our lives. There is every hope. You are not alone.
—Mary K.

One of the ideas behind the CRAFT approach is that parents and family members can help convince a person who is reluctant to go to treatment or get help. When I went to Boulder, Colorado, and discovered that my daughter was dependent on crystal meth, I was scared and had no idea where to turn. I was not familiar with addiction treatment programs—I had a lot of quick catching-up to do. I offer the following overview in the hope that if you need this information, you'll have the basics.

My daughter was nineteen at the time, and it seemed like her life had pretty much stalled out, so luckily she was willing to go to treatment. I felt that I had to act fast because things could change at a moment's notice.

If your child's situation is a life-threatening emergency, do get help immediately. When faced with the sense that you need to get your child to treatment immediately, the process can feel daunting. There are educational consultants and addiction counselors who can help, but be wary of people or websites who are funneling people into *their* treatment program regardless of whether it is the right fit for your child.

I've learned that if you have some time, research your options before you decide to place your child in a treatment program. Therapy with a counselor specializing in substance use can be an early option if your child is willing to go, depending on your child's situation and how far down the line they are with their drug or alcohol use.

Searching for a treatment center can be overwhelming. Not only are you dealing with the realization that your child is using drugs, but you may feel that your child's success in overcoming addiction is going to be based on the decisions that you make about treatment. That is a lot of pressure!

Yet, treatment can help your child. Your child can learn skills to live a healthier life. They can also dive into the root cause of the problem. Time well spent in a treatment program that meets your child's needs is valuable and even lifesaving.

Someone may have told you that your child has to want treatment for it to be effective, but even if your child is pressured or mandated to go into treatment, she still can have a successful experience. According to the National Institute on Drug Abuse, "Most studies suggest that outcomes for those who are legally pressured to enter treatment are as good as or better than outcomes for those who entered treatment without legal pressure. Individuals under legal pressure also tend to have higher attendance rates and remain in treatment for longer periods, which can also have a positive impact on treatment outcomes."

First Steps

You might start with having your child talk with their doctor or an addiction specialist if they are willing. It is essential to have a clear understanding about your child's physical condition and if detox is needed before entering treatment. Not all doctors are familiar with addiction issues; if they're not, ask them to refer you to a reputable addiction medicine professional.

Decide what kind of treatment you are seeking. Weigh the pros and cons of inpatient vs. outpatient treatment. If your child is under 18, look for a treatment center that works with teenagers.

Your child may prefer an all-male or all-female treatment center, or one that has experience with their particular identities—for example if they have mental health issues, LGBTQI+, or a person of color. Some of the obstacles facing these communities can be discrimination and social stigma. Co-occurring disorders and the need for specialized treatment options can also be a challenge, but there are more programs available to meet the needs of your son or daughter.

You can also contact your state health agency to find a list of treatment programs in your state. The SAMHSA Behavioral Health Treatment Locator is a place to search for treatment programs. The American Society of Addiction Medicine website lists addiction medicine physicians and addiction psychiatrists.

Therapists and Support Groups

Psychology Today is a place to get started with finding a therapist who specializes in addiction. Also, SMART Recovery meetings are sometimes led by therapists. They may be able to help you with some references to get you started finding a counselor. Friends and family can be another resource if they have sent a young person to a treatment program. The beauty of support groups is that you can ask other parents about their experience with a treatment program after the meeting, with the understanding that everyone is different. What might work for one person may not be the right fit for your child. But you can get some ideas and again, talking with others can help you get you started.

Finances are a problem for many parents when considering a treatment program for their child. This is not usually something you plan on or budget for. Check your local county services and see what they have to offer. There are low-cost treatment centers as well as free treatment available. But with any program, ask questions and do your best to see if the program will be a good fit for your child.

Finding a Good Fit

The thought of sending your child off to treatment with no guarantees can be daunting. If you do have a few programs to consider, do your homework. Find out as much as possible about what kind of therapy they provide and how much individual therapy your child will receive. Before choosing an addiction treatment center, educate yourself as much as possible about the different treatment programs available.

First, you'll need to decide between inpatient or outpatient options. Many people cannot afford or don't have the time to drop everything and attend a residential treatment program. For them, outpatient care offers the best alternative.

For others, relocating temporarily to a facility allows them to let go of all the distractions in their life and focus solely on their recovery. I know there were times when I just wanted to pluck my child out of their situation and put them safely away in a treatment program. Unfortunately, it's not quite that simple.

Inpatient centers can be expensive. You can ask if the treatment center is willing to negotiate the price and if any scholarships are available. Many centers also have payment plans that make it a little easier.

Before you start researching, it's good to have a clear sense of what you can afford. Be willing to investigate resources that are local as well as further away, as there are pros and cons to both. And what will be covered by your insurance? This may narrow things down for you too.

Be wary of having your child in a cookie-cutter treatment program where there is only one approach. There is no "right" way for someone to recover. There are many avenues to recovery, so hopefully the program you choose will support several options.

It's a missed opportunity when we don't meet our children where they are. Unfortunately, too many programs today still have just one approach. Ask questions and find out as much as you can about how the program works. It has taken a while, but slowly treatment programs are starting to realize that one size doesn't fit all. Yet there is so much more work to be done. And it starts with you asking for a program that uses research-based strategies, which will meet your child's needs.

Be sure as well to ask about the education background of the counselors. While people in recovery can be helpful, the program should be providing credentialed counselors, whether they are in recovery themselves or not.

It's my hope that more options will continue to be made available for those struggling with substances. An inpatient treatment program can be helpful, and you may want to consider options like harm reduction, an outpatient program, or counseling before deciding that inpatient treatment is necessary.

Our Treatment Stories

We called an educational consultant, which adds to the cost, but when I sent my daughter to a wilderness program, I felt reassured that the counselor had checked out the program. My son and I toured a treatment program to get help with marijuana use, but he decided to go with counseling instead.

My daughter's treatment began with the wilderness program in Utah. She then went to a women's program in southern California and decided to stay in their sober living facility for six months. Then she lived in an apartment with a friend from her sober living home while she finished college and worked. She eventually looked for a full-time job after graduating from college.

For six years, she was eight hours away from home and from those who might tempt her back into drug use. I feel sure that the length of her stay was the key to her success in recovery and living a healthier lifestyle. She has since told me that she most likely would have relapsed if she had come home after her five weeks in the wilderness program. I know this is not doable for every situation, but think through what is going to be the best environment for your son or daughter.

The Dangers of Relapse

I've heard of too many cases where a son or daughter comes home after a thirty-day treatment program and relapses soon after. You don't want to create a revolving door of treatment programs—that's costly and highly stressful for all involved.

If your son or daughter has decided to go to treatment, carving out a good chunk of time for a program can give them the best chance for long-term change. Another option is to go to treatment and then to an aftercare facility such as a sober living home. They have been at their drug or alcohol use for a while—it's going to take time to gain the internal strength to get their life back. Do your best to not cut the process short.

And unfortunately, relapse can often be part of the recovery process. It does not necessarily mean failure. Many things can trigger a relapse, including stress from work or family problems, encountering people from their past who are still using drugs, or driving by a place where they used to use. Even a smell associated with alcohol or drug use can trigger a relapse. So expect that relapse may be part of the process. Think through ahead of time what your options will be if a relapse occurs. That will help you deal with a relapse if it should happen. You can be a positive support and help your child get back on track. Do what you can do to support a situation that will give your child the best chance for long-term change.

Opioids and Medication

One cautionary note about early recovery. Carrie Wilkens, PhD, co-founder and clinical director of CMC: Foundation for Change and the Center for Motivation and Change, explains, "Opioids affect the central nervous system directly and, in high enough doses, cause respiratory depression and even death. This overdose risk is highest when people with opioid dependence have reduced tolerance after being detoxed from opioids, either through detoxification or incarceration. After a period of abstinence from them, a person's tolerance returns to zero. If they use again, they are at risk for using too much as they often figure, 'The last time I got high I needed X amount to feel high, so I should use that much now.' That amount with no tolerance floods their central nervous system and they stop breathing: an overdose."

Medications are available to help patients who are already abstinent to curb their craving for drugs or alcohol. These medications reduce the chances of relapse. Medicines prescribed by a doctor, with the addition of therapy, can help with long-term change. A support system of people who are on a similar path also sets them up for success.

Treatment Can Work

Consider your situation and what is going to work in the long run. While you may want your child home for special events or holidays, coming home too soon can often result in your child reverting to their old ways. It's sometimes better to connect with a phone call instead of a visit, so they have a better chance of a long-term healthy outcome. You know what is best for your situation.

Choosing a treatment program can take a leap of faith, but know that you are not alone. Treatment can work. Your child can get their life back, and you can get your child back.

Recovery

For many parents, it can be bittersweet when your son or daughter goes to treatment. Finally, you can breathe and not worry 24/7. Your child is under someone else's watch, and you can take a break. And you can have hope that your child will change.

You may expect that your child feels the same. You might assume that they are relieved about the new path they are on—and yet often there are mixed emotions. They may be ambivalent about both substance use and early recovery.

Don't Underestimate the Struggle

You might be surprised to learn that your son or daughter misses drug or alcohol use. They might miss the lifestyle, or even the rush they got when trying to obtain the drugs.

Your kid will need to find new friends who will support their recovery. That is a loss, and it isn't always easy. I've talked to a few parents whose children—in the prime of their lives—are genuinely alone because they've had to let go of old drug connections but do not yet have a sober community.

One of the great benefits of any group meeting is that there are opportunities every day to connect with others and not feel so alone. Your child can reach out to others, to help them move forward on those days when they are tired or wavering. Being surrounded by people on the same path can help any change process. Don't underestimate what you are asking your child to do.

Accept their feelings as part of the process. Let them know that you are there for them, even if their feelings scare you. Be a positive presence.

Early Recovery Is Hard

Early recovery doesn't always feel good. Diane, whose story we heard earlier, was disappointed in the early days of her son's recovery because he was crabby, which she didn't expect. She had thought he would be in a great mood.

Others seem to do fine once they've made up their mind that they want to change, but it's a process and not something that happens overnight. One of the things that keeps people from thinking about reducing their drug use or quitting is that it will likely take a while before they feel better. There is no instant gratification. It's a process.

What can help is parents not only focusing on their child's recovery but also on their change process. You may realize that it will feel freeing to let go of what you know is out of your control. Change is a project for everyone involved.

Throughout your child's early recovery process, the more you embrace self-care as a lifelong project, the better off you'll be. Trying to deal with my family's substance use stands out as one of the most complex experiences of my life. Things have gotten better, but I feel I will always need to be vigilant about my own healthy habits, so as not to slip back into old, unhealthy ones.

You may feel that you are now at a fork in the road where your child may (or may not) embrace change, and your fear may resurface. Parents usually have great anxiety when their child is in the midst of their use. Then they may get a break from that when they're in treatment. When their child is in the early change process, the fears may return—that they will slip up and relapse. It is understandable.

Focus on Yourself

While you may feel your happiness and well-being depend on what your child does or doesn't do, the more you can focus on yourself and your happiness, the better. Your child being happy, whole, and healthy may feel like the key to your happiness, and yet when you do your inner work, you can find happiness no matter what your child does. And the more you work on yourself, the better off your child will be—now and in the future.

You will then become a role model for your child. She will see you not just as her parent, but as a strong person who can weather the storms that life throws at her. She will also be able to loosen the burden of guilt that she feels because of all the pain she caused. Maybe she'll make amends for her previous actions—and then again, maybe she won't. Sometimes the shame may feel too great.

As Ron Grover, parent and creator of the blog An Addict in Our Son's Bedroom, states, "Never miss an opportunity to extend a hand to someone struggling with addiction or alcoholism. You never know when it is their time to enter recovery. Recovery works. The love you show may be the straw that tips the scale."

Chapter Summary

- Treatment can help your child. Your child can learn skills to live a healthier life.
- Learn as much as you can about treatment programs. Do your best to see if they will meet the needs of your child.

- Relapse can often be part of the recovery process. It does not necessarily mean failure.
- Medications are available to help curb cravings for drugs and alcohol. These medications reduce the chances of relapse and should be made available to your child through a medical professional.
- Your child can get their life back, and you can get your child back.

CHAPTER 11

Hope and Happiness

Not only am I still standing, but I know more and feel more than I once thought was possible. —David Sheff

It helps to know you are not alone, as well as having resilience and strength to go another day with encouragement... Humor also helps. Mindfulness and meditation help, as does exercise—all things I need to practice more... Hang in there and keep practicing and loving your family. —Joy R.

What I discovered, and I believe the other parents did as well, on that first parent CRAFT training in August 2013, is that CRAFT offers a path forward for struggling families. It is an approach that truly gives hope for the future that everyone can feel good about.

While this is a difficult time, know that growth can occur during times of crisis. Although we all wish that life could go along peacefully, there are always bumps in the road. Sometimes when we are struggling, we have to be reminded to be grateful. It is so easy to get caught up in the chaos of others around us, especially as related to our kids, regardless of their age.

But we learn from our challenges and setbacks. They are what make us who we are. We heal and find joy when we look for something positive, even when things are not going well. We look for the bright spots when our kids go through challenges.

Gratitude

Dealing with our kids' substance use is difficult. There is no getting around that. Yet when you find yourself consumed with the problem and lose sight of things to be grateful for, it makes it more challenging to move forward.

As I talk to parents of children with substance use issues, I am reminded of how important gratitude is. Tremendous growth can occur when we are struggling. Our life can change for the better.

Here are some things parents who have a struggling child are grateful for on any given day:

- "I'm thankful that my daughter was sober yesterday."
- "I'm grateful that my son is becoming more resilient and independent."
- "My son entered a long-term sober living facility yesterday."
- "I'm thankful my daughter is in sober living and in a good state of mind."
- "My daughter completed an inpatient treatment program and has come home with hope and pride. She seems serious about her sober life."
- "I'm grateful that my son is still alive and working toward getting his life back."

No matter what our situation is, we can all find something to be grateful for. Even if you feel confused or troubled, know that every experience in your life can offer a gift—even if you can't see it yet. See if you can look at each situation with eyes of gratitude. It may be an opportunity to grow and be creative. You will be stronger for what you have been through.

When you feel fear because of your child's substance use, take a moment and notice the growth in your life. Instead of letting fear stop you in your tracks, look back and be grateful for how much progress you have made. Feel the strength of your growth.

Think back on the many gifts your life has brought you. It helps to find joy in the simple things you can be thankful for during this challenging time.

Acknowledge those close to you, and tell them often how much you appreciate and love them. Take a moment out of your day to say thank you. When you give joy to others, you will feel better yourself.

I've realized that gratitude is at the core of my happiness. Even if you have a child who struggles with substance use, you can still feel happiness. Gratitude can still have a place in your life.

As you train your mind to look for the positive, a shift may evolve. One thing that has helped me make the shift is to list a few things I'm grateful for every day, whether I'm feeling like it or not. It is a great reminder to see what you are thankful for in writing, and to look back on everything you've listed on days past.

As you shift your gaze, you may even find yourself no longer caught up in the negative cycle of what's happening around you. The understandable stress around your child's behavior will hopefully lessen. You can find your inner strength and learn how to stop being the one who suffers.

Life Is a Gift

When we have moments of crisis in our life, it is essential to acknowledge the sorrow and pain. It is also important to work through the process and allow something beautiful to evolve. There is nothing more beautiful than seeing young men and women who have changed their lives and have gone on into their futures with meaning and purpose.

You can turn your anger into calm, despair into joy, doubt into hope, resentment into compassion, frustration into acceptance, and shame into empowerment. You can live your life in a meaningful way, even during hard times. When you take care of yourself, strive to have positive conversations with your struggling child, use positive reinforcement, allow consequences, and set clear boundaries, the chances that your child will change will be far greater.

Life is a gift. Even if you feel confused or troubled, know that every life experience can offer an opportunity to grow and start anew. You can weather this storm. Growth can occur when we are struggling. Grab that opportunity and change your life for the better.

Notice the miracles that have touched your life. Sometimes when we are struggling, it is easy to forget or overlook the subtle stuff. Now is an excellent time to remind yourself to be thankful for the little things in life that bring daily beauty and joy. When you can, notice the gifts of nature that surround you. The soft wind, the ripples in the lake, or the sound of the birds can be calming.

The Silver Bullet

Each one of you reading this book has your own story to tell. Many of the details are likely far more intriguing than mine. My two kids, who struggled with substance use for years—after bumps in the road, and some starts and stops—have gone on to find themselves. They still have ups and downs, of course, and their lives are still challenging from time to time. But they are managing well and are better people because of their past experiences. Through it all, my three children have been my greatest joys.

I feel blessed that we are all moving forward. What I've learned is that there are no easy answers. We are all on a learning curve, trying to find our way.

A mom recently asked me if I had found the silver bullet yet. We kidded back and forth about when the silver bullet will be arriving. As you know by now, there is no silver bullet for addiction. There is no guarantee that we can change our child's behavior, but our actions can influence their behavior and give them a better chance at change.

As parents, we're role models for our kids. Our actions, often more than our words, will be what our children learn and remember. It's how we make our kids feel that's key. We are leaders in helping our kids, no matter what their age, to overcome their drug or alcohol use. With gentle guidance, we can motivate them to change.

Hope for the Future

In the years to come, I hope that awareness and education about substance use will spread. I hope that parents of teens will help their children live a healthy lifestyle, that they'll start and continue the conversation about the dangers of drug use. If we all pitch in to help spread awareness, the kids of the future will have a better chance.

As we look to the future, I am amazed by the progress many families have made. There's nothing more rewarding than having a parent write to let me know that their child is living a healthier life. If you are a parent of a struggling young adult or teen, you can be the change igniter. It can be as simple as listening and being present for your son or daughter.

Many Roads to Recovery

You will hear many opinions about what you should do when it comes to helping your child. It is good to have a variety of opinions. Families looking for support must have access to different options to make effective decisions. Yet in the end, this is your child and your family. Listen to what your heart is telling you is the right thing to do.

Sometimes it is the right time to reach out and give your child that extra support they need to make the decision to seek help. Sometimes it's meeting your child for a cup of coffee or a meal and talking about something other than their substance use. Other times you may be feeling overwhelmed and in need of a break.

There are many situations that come up when you are trying to help your child change. Your situation may be similar to others', yet we all have our own unique path. There are many roads to recovery.

Please don't allow the stigma of addiction to keep you from getting help. Find people who have walked in your shoes and understand your pain. The more you bring your child's substance use out into the open with people you trust, the more you will reduce the stigma and shame you feel.

I've learned that whenever I bring up my family's struggle with substance use, at least one person in the room knows someone who has the same issue. Addiction is everywhere. If we are open, we learn we are not alone.

Looking to the Future

As we move toward the future, let's work together to reduce the number of people affected by substance use. Let's share our stories, so drugs and alcohol have less power to sideline our children during the critical adolescent years.

We need to make research-based, proven approaches available to families at all economic levels. Treatment should be available for everyone. It is an expensive problem for our communities, so we've got to put time and effort into figuring out answers that make sense.

The issue that continues to be at the heart of addiction is teen drug and alcohol use. I would love to see more government dollars put toward prevention, because that is the key to helping our kids stay safe.

As you can see, there is much work to be done. Let's shine a light on this problem—so we can come together, use up-to-date approaches, spread awareness, and lessen the stigma. Let's bring these complicated shadows out of the dark.

My Hope for You

When you feel stressed and start thinking about giving up, know that there is hope for your child. He or she *can* recover and go on to thrive. Many have worked their way through an addiction that has had a stranglehold on them. Hang on to hope, and know that one step at a time, you can get where you want to go.

When I was feeling hopeless and didn't know where to turn, believing that somehow, some way, my child's life would turn around for the better was the one thing that got me up in the morning.

I've heard many addiction stories and I know the toll that it can take on a human mind and body. Our kids need support, time, and love. They need our compassion every step of the way. When you change the conversation, and lean in with understanding and kindness, change can unfold.

You can help get your young adult or teen get back on track. Keep reaching out, find ways to help, and keep them close. Remember who your child once was and who they can become.

You can thrive as well. With hope for the future and compassion for yourself, you will be able to pick up the pieces and move forward—more empowered, wise, and confident.

ACKNOWLEDGMENTS

As I think back over the years that I've worked with parents of struggling young adults and teens, I want to acknowledge the strength, courage, and determination that so many parents have to help their children live a healthy life. Thank you to my clients who have shared their hearts and their lives with me. I'm honored to have walked beside you. One of the most rewarding parts of this journey has been meeting so many incredible people.

I want to thank Robert J. Meyers for having the wisdom and foresight to create Community Reinforcement and Family Training (CRAFT), so that families have access to an evidence-based, compassionate, kind approach to help their loved ones. CRAFT has changed many lives for the better.

Thank you to Jeff Foote, PhD, Carrie Wilkens, PhD, Nicole Kosanke, PhD, Ken Carpenter, PhD, Josh King, PhD, and all the psychologists at the CMC: Foundation for Change and the Center for Motivation and Change. Thank you as well to Meg Murray. The support from CMC of families through your work, books and foundation has been invaluable.

What foresight the Partnership to End Addiction had to partner with CMC for parent coach training and to create the Parent Coaching Network. Thank you for being so dedicated to helping parents when your support is so greatly needed. Thank you to the late

Tom Hendrick, Kevin Collins, Madison Moore, Denise Mariano, and all the other people at the Partnership for the work that you are doing.

Also, thank you to Teja Watson, my editor, Jessica Schmidt, who also helped with the editing of this book, and Paula Hickey, who has been such a help with her creative talents. Thank you to all the parents who were early readers and supporters and to the parents who shared their quotes and experiences. This book wouldn't have happened without you. I am indebted to you and appreciate your input.

Finally, my family is always where my heart will be. Thank you to my husband and my three children for all of your support. We never expected to be here, but here we are. We are better people because of our experiences and challenges. As we go forward, we can look back with much gratitude.

ABOUT THE AUTHOR

As a result of her journey with her own child's drug use, Catherine Taughinbaugh, a former educator, became a certified parent coach. Catherine is one of more than three hundred Community Reinforcement and Family Training (CRAFT) Parent Network Coaches trained by the Center for Motivation and Change and the Partnership to End Addiction.

Catherine is also a Certified Parent Coach through the Parent Coach Trainers Academy, Certified Life Coach from the Life Coach Institute of Orange County. She has a Certificate of Completion from Robert J. Meyers's Community Reinforcement and Family Training (CRAFT) and from the Training in the Invitation to Change Approach with the American Academy of Addiction Psychiatry.

She is the founder of the Regain Your Hope video course and support community for parents who are struggling because of their child's substance use. Catherine is a graduate of the University of the Pacific, with a degree in psychology.

Visit her blog: www.cathytaughinbaugh.com/blog

Visit her website: www.cathytaughinbaugh.com

NOTES

Introduction

According to the, National Association of Addiction Treatment Providers, Addiction & Treatment Resources, https://www.naatp.org/addiction-treatment-resources.

Chapter 1

I learn so much, Grover, Ron, "An Addict in Our Son's Bedroom," https://parentsofanaddict.blogspot.com/.

In 2013, the Partnership offered, Partnership to End Addiction, https://drugfree.org/get-support/.

Chapter 2

It's a sad fact that my article, CathyTaughinbaugh.com, "When Addiction Wins," https://cathytaughinbaugh.com/when-addiction-wins-support-for-grieving-families/, August 27, 2020.

However its rise in the rankings, National Institute on Drug Abuse, Overdose Death Rates, https://www.drugabuse.gov/drug-topics/trends-statistics/overdose-death-rates, January 29, 2021.

According to the, Partnership to End Addiction, https://drugfree.org/article/how-worried-should-i-be-about-my-childs-drug-use/, September 2020.

While trauma can be the root cause, Centers for Disease Control and Prevention, About the CDC-Kaiser ACE Study, https://www.cdc.gov/violenceprevention/aces/about.html.

According to, Hartney, Elizabeth, Bsc., MSc.MA, PHD, Is Tough Love Affective in Treating Addiction?, Very Well Mind, https://www.verywellmind.com/what-is-tough-love-22418.

There are many, Partnership to End Addiction, https://drugfree.org/article/risk-factors-problem-use-addiction/, April, 2021.

Chapter 3

Studies conducted by, Meyers, Robert J. PhD, Wolfe, Brenda L. PhD., *Get Your Loved One Sober: Alternatives to Nagging, Pleading, and Threatening, (Hazelden Publishing, 2004), pgs. xvii - xix.*

CRAFT has, Foote, Jeffrey PhD, Wilkens, Carrie PhD, and Kosanke, Nicole PhD with Stephanie Higgs, (2014) *Beyond Addiction: How Science and Kindness Help People Change,* (New York, Scribner), pg. 6-7.

Jeff Foote, PhD, CathyTaughinbaugh.com, "CRAFT Can Help Your Family Change: Meet Dr. Jeffrey Foote," https://cathytaughinbaugh.com/craft-can-help-your-family-change-meet-dr-jeff-foote/, December 15, 2013.

I wanted to know about, Grosso, Chris, *Dead Set On Living: Making the Difficult but Beautiful Journey from F#*king Up to Waking Up* (Gallery Books, March 6, 2018), pg. 25.

According to, Jaffe, Adi, PhD, CampusSpeak, “Shame Is One Hell of an Emotion,” https://campuspeak.com/shame-one-hell-emotion/.

The research of, Miller, Emmett, MD, The Power of Forgiveness – A Conversation with Frederic Luskin, PhD, https://www.drmiller.com/luskin/.

Chapter 4

In his book, Hampton, Ryan, *American Fix: Inside the Opioid Addiction Crisis—And How to End It* (All Points Books, 2018) pg. 235.

Ten Deep Breaths, Harris, Dr. Russ, *The Happiness Trap: How to Stop Struggling and Start Living,* (Trumpeter Books, 2011), pg. 67-68.

In the Artist's Way, Cameron, Julia, *The Artist's Way: A Spiritual Path to Higher Creativity,* (G.P. Putnam's Sons New York, 1992). pg. 10, pg. 15.

In his book Writing to Heal, Allyson Latta.ca, Dr. James Pennebaker (on writing to heal), https://www.allysonlatta.ca/interview/more-interviews/conversation-with-dr-james-pennebaker/, 2009.

Dr. Pennebaker explains, Pennebaker, PhD, James W. and Smyth, PhD, Joshua M., *Opening Up by Writing It Down: How Expressive Writing Improves Health and Eases Emotional Pain,* (The Guilford Press, 2016), pg. 26.

Dr. Pennebaker goes on to say, Pennebaker, PhD, James W. and Smyth, PhD, Joshua M., *Opening Up by Writing It Down: How Expressive Writing Improves Health and Eases Emotional Pain,* (The Guilford Press, 2016), pg. 166.

I listened to an episode, Bell, Dr. Herby, Sober Conversations, Wellness and Thriving in Recovery, Episode 5, "Addiction in the Family - A Father's Story," https://soberconversations.life/.

Not to be confused with self-pity, Hampton, Debbie, "The Benefits of Self-Compassion and How to Get More", https://www.thebestbrainpossible.com/the-benefits-of-self-compassion-and-how-to get-more/, June 2016.

According to, Kristin Neff, PhD, *Self-Compassion: The Proven Power of Being Kind to Yourself* (HarperCollins: 2011), pg. 41.

Chapter 5

In his book, Reedy, Brad, PhD, *The Journey of the Heroic Parent: Your Child's Struggle and the Road Home* (Regan Arts, 2015), pg. 34.

Dr. Robert Meyers explained, CathyTaughinbaugh.com, "How the Powerful CRAFT Approach Is Saving Lives: Meet Bob Meyers," https://cathytaughinbaugh.com/how-the-powerful-craft-approach-is-saving-lives-meet-bob-meyers/, October 22, 2015.

Chapter 6

Here are some parenting styles to consider., Parent Coach Training Academy, "Coaching for Parents of Struggling Teen and Young Adults," Chapter 8, Holding up the Mirror, 2014.

One in four children, Wallerstein, Julia S., Lewis, Julia M., and Blakeslee, Sandra, *The Unexpected Legacy of Divorce: The 25 Year Landmark Study,* (Hyperion, 2000), pg. 188.

Below are the, "Ten Basic Messages for Families," Robert J. Meyers, PhD & Associates, CRAFT, Community Reinforcement and Family Training, Boise, Idaho, 2015.

Ten Hard Things for Siblings, Clancy, Dawn, Fellowship Hall, "10 Things That Suck About Being an Addict's Sibling," https://www.fellowshiphall.com/2017/07/10-things-suck-addicts-sibling/, July 31, 2017.

Chapter 7

The Stages of Change Model, Proschaska, James O. PhD, Prochaska, Janice M. PhD, *Changing to Thrive: Using the Stages of Change to Overcome the Top Threats to Your Happiness and Happiness* (Hazelden Publishing, 2016), pg. ix.

Typical relapse rates, National Institute on Drug Abuse, Drugs, Brain and Behavior: The Science of Addiction, Treatment& Recovery, https://www.drugabuse.gov/publications/drugs-brains-behavior-science-addiction/treatment-recovery, July 2020.

Dr. Jonah Berger, author of, Berger, Jonah, *The Catalyst: How to Change Anyone's Mind* (Simon & Schuster; Illustrated edition, 2020), pg. 38.

According to, Berger, Jonah, *The Catalyst: How to Change Anyone's Mind* (Simon & Schuster; Illustrated edition, 2020), pg. 112.

According to, Clear, James, *Atomic Habits: An Easy & Proven Way to Build Good Habits & Break Bad Ones* (Avery, 2018), pg. 6.

Chapter 8

You may have seen a New York Times article, Foote, Jeffrey PhD, Wilkens, Carrie PhD, and Kosanke, Nicole, PhD with Higgs Stephanie, (2014) *Beyond Addiction: How Science and Kindness Help People Change,* (New York, Scribner, 2014), pg. 174.

The old saying, Meyers, Robert J. PhD, Wolfe, Brenda L. PhD, *Get Your Loved One Sober: Alternatives to Nagging, Pleading, and Threatening* (Hazelden Publishing, 2004), pg. 144.

As Dr. Meyers says, Meyers, *Robert J. PhD, Wolfe, Brenda L. PhD, Get Your Loved One Sober: Alternatives to Nagging, Pleading, and Threatening* (Hazelden Publishing, 2004), pg. 39.

Chapter 9

The Parent's 20 Minute Guide states, Center for Motivation and Change, *Parent's 20 Minute Guide,* 2013, pg. *99.*

Chapter 10

According to the, National Institute on Drug Abuse, Drugs, Brain and Behavior: The Science of Addiction, Treatment & Recovery, https://www.drugabuse.gov/publications/principles-drug-abuse-treatment-criminal-justice-populations-research-based-guide/legally-mandated-treatment-effective, April 2014.

The SAMHSA, Behavioral Health Treatment Services Locator, https://findtreatment.samhsa.gov/.

The American Society, The American Society of Addiction Medicine, https://www.asam.org/.

Psychology Today,
Psychology Today, https://www.psychologytoday.com/us.

Also, SMART Recovery, https://www.smartrecovery.org/.

One cautionary note, Megale, S.C., *American Boy: The Opioid Crisis and the Sister Left Behind*, with afterword by Wilkens, Carrie, PhD (Bluebullseye Press, 2019), pg. 134.

Never miss an opportunity, Grover, Ron, "Let It Ride", https://parentsofanaddict.blogspot.com/, July 6, 2019.

RESOURCES

Above the Influence
https://abovetheinfluence.com/

Addiction Education Society
https://addictioneducationsociety.org/

Affirming Our LGBTQ+ Youth
https://drugfree.org/how-to-protect-lgbtq-youth-from-the-risks-and-harm-of-substance-use/

The American Society of Addiction Medicine
https://www.asam.org/

Association of Recovery Schools
https://recoveryschools.org/

Behavioral Health Treatment Services Locator
https://findtreatment.samhsa.gov/

Beyond Addiction: How Science and Kindness Help People Change
Jeffrey Foote, PhD, Carrie Wilkens, Phd, Nicole Kosanke, PhD with Stephanie Higgs
This book. published in 2014, goes beyond the theatrics of interventions and tough love to show family and friends how they can

use kindness, positive reinforcement, and motivational and behavioral strategies to help someone change.

Breaking the Cycles
https://www.breakingthecycles.com/blog/

Center for Motivation Change
https://motivationandchange.com/

CMC:Foundation for Change
https://cmcffc.org/

College Parents Matter
http://www.collegeparentsmatter.org/

Get Your Love One Sober: Alternatives to Nagging, Pleading, and Threatening
Robert J. Meyers and Brenda L. Wolfe
This book, published in 2003, describes Community Reinforcement and Family Training (CRAFT), the program uses scientifically validated behavioral principles to reduce the loved one's substance use and to encourage him or her to seek treatment.

Helping Families Help: CRAFT Resources for families dealing with addiction
www.helpingfamilieshelp.com
https://www.soberfamilies.com/resources-for-families-dealing-with-addiction

Robert J. Meyers. PhD
https://robertjmeyersphd.com/

National Association of Therapeutic Schools and Programs (NATSAP)
https://natsap.org/

National Institute on Drug Abuse, NIDA
https://www.drugabuse.gov/

No-Cost Low-Cost Alcohol and Drug Treatment Directory
https://drug-addiction-help-now.org/2013/05/low-cost-no-cost-alcohol-drug-treatment/

Partnership to End Addiction
https://drugfree.org/

The Parent's 20 Minute Guide (Second Edition)
This book, published in 2016, was developed by psychologists at the Center for Motivation and Change. This guide helps parents change their child's substance use. There is a partner version as well. Read the book online here: https://the20minuteguide.com/

Regain Your Hope
This is a video course, support group and online community utilizing Community Reinforcement and Family Training (CRAFT)
https://cathytaughinbaugh.com/regain-your-hope/

SAMHSA Behavioral Health Treatment Locator
https://findtreatment.samhsa.gov

SUPPORT GROUPS

Al-Anon/Alateen
https://al-anon.org/

Alcoholics Anonymous
https://www.aa.org/

GRASP: Grief Recovery After a Substance Passing
http://grasphelp.org/

Life Ring
https://lifering.org/

Marijuana Anonymous
https://marijuana-anonymous.org/

Moderation Management
https://moderation.org/

Narcotics Anonymous
https://www.na.org/

Nar-Anon Family Groups
https://www.nar-anon.org/naranon/

Recovery Dharma
https://recoverydharma.org/

She Recovers (group support for women and specified groups)
https://sherecovers.org/together-online/

SMART Recovery
https://www.smartrecovery.org/

SMART Recovery Family & Friends
https://www.smartrecovery.org/family/

Women for Sobriety
https://womenforsobriety.org/